# Endorsements

"The author brings a simply delightful Southern twist to her thoughts and dialogue. It's like Paula Deen meets Dr. Oz. She offers helpful clinical information and just plain down home advice and insight."

"This book goes beyond a typical cancer survivor story. It brings humor and insight to breast reconstruction."

"Delightful Southern charm and voice!"

"She shares her thoughts, her tips for coping, and even her progress photos. What a rare gift to other women facing similar decisions and treatment."

"The book should appeal not only to patients but to their families, friends, and medical staff."

*iUniverse Editorial Evaluation Team*

"Well done! It's Magic..." Dr. Marcus H. Crawford

a.k.a. *Super Doc*

# Perky Mutant

## Melissa Brumbelow

*Breast wishes!*

*Melissa*

*1·19·2011*

iUniverse, Inc.
Bloomington

# Perky Mutant

The information, ideas, and suggestions in this book are not intended as a substitute for professional medical advice. Before following any suggestions contained in this book, you should consult your personal physician. Neither the author nor the publisher shall be liable or responsible for any loss or damage allegedly arising as a consequence of your use or application of any information or suggestions in this book.

iUniverse books may be ordered through booksellers or by contacting:

iUniverse
1663 Liberty Drive
Bloomington, IN 47403
www.iuniverse.com
1-800-Authors (1-800-288-4677)

Because of the dynamic nature of the Internet, any Web addresses or links contained in this book may have changed since publication and may no longer be valid. The views expressed in this work are solely those of the author and do not necessarily reflect the views of the publisher, and the publisher hereby disclaims any responsibility for them.

ISBN: 978-1-4502-6803-5 (sc)
ISBN: 978-1-4502-6877-6 (ebook)
ISBN: 978-1-4502-6878-3 (dj)

Library of Congress Control Number: 2010916056

Printed in the United States of America

iUniverse rev. date: 12/03/2010

# Acknowledgements to my cast of characters

For my husband, *Studly~* Thank you for your nose-lickings and bullfrogs. They are the best medicine ever.

For *I Love My OB-GYN All to Pieces* ~ thank you for saving my butt twice in a row. For my Oncologists; *Honey Doc* ~ for being so sweet & pink; *Gospel Doc* ~ for being a member of the family through 17 cancers and treating me like I was one of your own; *New York-New York*, for peaking at the fax machine.

For my true family; Mama ~ for understanding medicinal margaritas and bail money go hand in hand, Daddy ~ for never giving me a single ounce of bad advice and teaching me scars give character, Nana ~ for teaching me pain doesn't last - may your chicken salad reign forever, The Gang & The Nukes ~ for friendships that radiate support.

For *Super Doc* ~ thank you for swooping down in your white cape and keeping it real; for an *Amazing Admin* who can run that office with hands tied behind her back & blindfolded; a *Lovely Assistant* from one home girl to another; *Mama Anesthesia* and *Just Joe* for knocking me out and running for cover when I woke up.

*Thanks, Y'all!*

# Psychobabble

**OB-GYN** (abbv. & noun) the person who straps you to a table, places your feet high in stirrups, and uses tools on your body you would otherwise consider kinky

- **BRCA1 & 2** (abbv. & noun) Breast Cancer 1 (dealing mostly with chromosome 13) and Breast Cancer 2 (chromosome 17) genes found on your DNA strand
- **Mutation** (adj.) A change of the DNA sequence within a gene or chromosome of an organism resulting in the creation of a new character usually involving a theme song or costume
- **Gene** (noun) the dot on either side of the DNA strand that looks like the rungs on a ladder
- **DNA** (noun) the twisted strands of ladders floating around in your body that make you who you are

**Oncologist** (noun) fancy name for a cancer doctor that is usually misspelled by anyone who's never dealt with this doctor before

- **Ultrasound** (noun) warm jelly, a magic wand, and a weird looking tv that shows pictures of the inside of your squishy organs
- **Mammogram** (noun) acrylic plates, and x-ray images that result from flat boobs. Usually involves cold hands

- *MRI* (noun) bigger version of a mammogram, only this time the machine buzzes

*Reconstructive Surgeon* (noun) someone specializing in helping a mutant look normal again

- *Latisimus Dorsi Bilateral Mastectomy* (pronoun) where the third lat muscles in your back are cut from near the spine, wrapped back around the front side of your rib cage, and are reattached to the front of your breast bone. This ride not recommended for the faint hearted.
- *Skin flap* (noun) circle shaped piece of your own skin from your back, removed during the Latisimus Dorsi Bilateral Mastectomy, and stitched to whatever amount of skin is left over on the front side where your nipples used to be *(sort of like looking at a dog without a nose...something ain't right)*
- *Expander Implants* (pronoun) water balloons installed under your remaining breast tissue the Reconstructive Surgeon can fill-up once a week until you spring a leak
- *Injection* (noun) a large animal Vet sized needle and syringe used to fill-up the expander implants
- *Permanent Implants* (noun) installed after the expander implants have done their job, and are made out of a substance known as Memory Gel...the memory is how they remember to keep their shape
- *Drain tubes* (noun) uncomfortable plastic tubing sprouting from your back and sides like spider legs after a mastectomy to suck the bad fluids away

*Anesthesiologist* (noun) your new best friend when surgery time rolls around

# Chapters

# I Love My OB-GYN All to Pieces ~ Takin' the tests & getting' the results

Imagine you are 28 years old, rocking a sexy new business suit from work, heading to meet your *studly* husband as soon as the next appointment for the day is over with for date night, and you're healthy as a horse. That next appointment is the annual visit to the OB-GYN. Every woman just loves that yearly check-up. Y'all know the one I'm talking about – the one that includes stirrups, cattle prods, hotter than branding iron hot flashes, and what once was round is squished flatter than a pancake.

Well this past March, my OB-GYN added another lil' tid bit to the party. I sat high in the stirrups as she told me about a new test for women ages 25-45 years old called the BRCAnalysis Test (bra-ka) and it was specifically for women with a lot of cancer in their families. Well cancer in my family is profound. We have seventeen cases of cancer in my immediate family alone, immediate being my grandparents, parents, aunts and uncles, and first cousins.

Most people know someone else that has cancer or might have one or two cases somewhere in their gene pool; however, not seventeen cases in their immediate family alone. My paternal grandfather was the first diagnosed back in 1989; colon cancer took almost seven years to beat back into remission before rearing its ugly head again at the tenth year and spreading from his colon into his spine, bone marrow, brain and lungs. He passed away Christmas time of 1999.

My paternal grandmother was diagnosed in the spring of 1991 with breast cancer, and she chose to undergo a unilateral (one sided) mastectomy vs. a lumpectomy which would then also require chemotherapy and radiation. Her reason she stated, was that she had a husband undergoing surgeries, chemo, and radiation already; she didn't have time to waste on herself if she didn't absolutely have to.

Talk about one helluva strong woman, like those stong pioneer women you see in the ol' westerns. She didn't blink an eye, had her Oncologist remove the left breast, and as quick as she could recover she was tending to my grandfather again. Within ten years, her breast cancer came back full force and spread to her sternum and her spine. She passed away in late summer of 2004.

My maternal grandmother also was diagnosed with breast cancer back in 2001. She was able to have her cancer removed with a lumpectomy and took chemo and radiation afterwards. Nana is still receiving the all clear signs from her Oncologist to this day! Aunts and uncles have had everything from ovarian, uterine, prostate, and skin cancers throughout the past decade or so.

My *I Love My OB-GYN All to Pieces* knew our family history and so did I, and she wanted me to take this test whether insurance paid for it or not. Turns out you must 'qualify' in order to take this test, meaning you have to have certain amounts of cancer trickling down the branches of your family tree or else insurance won't pay. It's unfortunate that we think in today's economy of money over health, and what insurance will or will not pay for. It is; however, the truth. I asked about just how much this test would cost and what I could expect from my insurance company as far as help was concerned. *I Love My OB-GYN All to Pieces* informed me that the test itself cost approximately three thousand dollars.

In addition, within the past year, the federal and state governments had passed health bills to ensure if you took this test no future insurance would be denied and she even had this information printed out for me as well as brochures. Therefore, before I asked her more questions she steered me back in the right direction of just what took place during this BRCAnalysis testing. There in her office, they would draw five vials of blood and send them specially packaged to the genetic laboratories. She explained the procedures to me. Their lab techs would test my blood for the five genetic hereditary cancers known to women, and they would send back my results on a piece of paper. Those cancers were breast, ovarian, pancreatic, stomach and colon. There would be BRCA-1 and BRCA-2 results listed on the same report and I would literally have a list of percentages typed out in black and white right before my eyes, letting me know what my chances really were based on the mutated genes found linked to my DNA.

Whew – that's a lot of brutal information in a short period, so let's get a good grip on this and simplify what is going to happen: five vials of blood drawn and sent to the lab, they put it under a microscope and pinpoint the mutated genes in your DNA strands to verify the existence of hereditary cancers. It's amazing how far medical science has come to give you such detailed results, which sounded like cancer's crystal ball to me, giving me a glimpse in the future so I took this opportunity.

A few weeks after the bloodletting, *I Love My OB-GYN All to Pieces* called to let me know my results were in and my doctor wanted to speak to me. Oh, boy…I'm thinking to myself if it was good news the office would've sent me a note in the mail…I felt like I was being called into the principal's office for misbehaving. I had visions of bad news and when I showed up, *I Love My OB-GYN All to Pieces* pulls out my file, and we sat down to sure enough have what us Southerners' call a come-to-Jesus-meeting.

Now I knew my results weren't going to be all that good, because of my family history of cancers. I just wasn't prepared for my percentages, listed on that report. I tested 87 percent positive for breast cancer and 44 percent positive for ovarian cancer, both by the age of 40, with a 20 percent chance of the cancer recurring in less than 4 years if I opted for chemo and radiation.

Y'all, I just wasn't ready to hear numbers that ginormous! Good grief – I thought percentages of 5-15 percent were big – I never expected a number as large as 87 percent! A percentage that big is like a creek so full it's almost spilling over the dam, it's a 401K you've invested in for years almost fully vested, and it's even an age way older than my grandmother! Moreover, let's just add a scoop of ovarian cancer with a cherry on top while we're at it, why don't we.

I got nervous to say the least, and when that happens I can't help but crack jokes to remove the tension. I sat there for a few seconds staring between my *I Love My OBGYN All to Pieces* and that one piece of paper before finally saying,

"So my genes are mutated 87 and 44 percent."

*I Love My OBGYN All to Pieces* looks straight at me and says a direct, "Yes."

"So what you're telling me is that I'm a MUTANT."

Her eyes twinkle and her lip twitches in the upper corner and she says, "Absolutely, and don't you even think of coming into my office wearing a costume to prove it!"

Now you can't digest that kind of information in your allotted appointment time at the doctor's office. The shock of this news will rock your boat for quite a while; however, there was some good news if you can call it good news after hearing this verdict: I did not show any signs of abby-normal developments in pap-smears or mammograms, so right now I felt initially I was safe. I knew I had done the right thing.

Taking the test and waiting for the results of the report was the hardest part, but step #1 was complete. Step #2 meant I was headed to the family oncologists and other specialists so the doctor's could sync up each year to keep a better eye on me now that we knew exactly what was coming in the not-so-distant future.

Nothing could be done but I needed to tell someone...the most important person in my life...my husband, *Studly*. I made sure my game face was on, kept my facts straight from my emotions when we talked, and just told it like it was because there is no other way to do it. If you know anything about me, then you know this is not an easy task on my part.

When I got home and let loose, we both immediately teared up with the fear of the unknown but almost certainty of facing cancer and from memories of past warriors, some of whom lost the struggle to beat the disease, and in honor of current survivors in our families. We sucked it up and knew what we had to do – make the first available appointment with my family's oncology group.

# Forming A Game-plan
## *Cancer won't bond to silicone!*

In just a few days time, I had my appointment. That's the fastest service in the medical industry I had ever experienced; turns out *I Love My OB-GYN All to Pieces* lit up the phone lines of the oncologist's office and broke the news and made arrangements before I could….did I mention *I Love My OB-GYN All to Pieces*?

*Studly* and I went to the appointment with the expectation of developing a long term plan of monitoring my health with *Honey Doc* (my Oncologist, because she's the sweetest thing and pink as can be) about forming a game plan over the next 10 yrs or so, what all they would do, etc. We were told once a year around the same time as my annual physical, I would simply come into their office and they would order additional blood work, MRIs of my breasts and ovaries, and stay on top of this issue so that when something should develop we were locked-stocked-and ready for battle. This service sounded awesome to *Studly* and I, because at this point we were just in awe of the amount of medical attention and analysis, we'd received in such a short time period.

As we were handed the booklets and brochures on BRCA-1 and BRCA-2 analysis, *Honey Doc* asked if while I was in her office if it would be alright for her to do her own breast exam. I said sure, and off we went to put on a lovely paper evening gown – the one that's cut real low in the front.

She laid me back and was literally holding up my mammogram images in her left hand while examining me with her right hand. She got really quiet, dreadfully still, and she seemed concerned. She poked, prodded, and pushed until I thought she'd pop my left lung and then she said, "Oh-My-God."

Words you never want to hear your doctor say. She walked around the exam table, flipped on the ultra-sound machine, grabbed warm jelly, squirted it on my boobs, and went to town pressing down what wasn't flat already. The anticipation was getting to me when she finally mentioned we had a genuine problem because she *felt* multiple lumps in my left breast that didn't show up a month and a half ago on my mammogram.

It doesn't take a rocket scientist to figure out that if nothing was there a month ago, and has grown big enough to feel, that it's aggressive. Then she told me something I will never forget. She said, "I'm sorry Sweet Pea, this is the beginning – you don't have time for a 10 year game plan – it is here now and we've got to get it before it gets you."

Well, that was all it took for my poker face to melt into a million pieces and slide right down my lap and into the floor along with my heart. When I looked at my Studly sitting in the chair and our glances met, I knew that his feelings mirrored my own. If we thought we weren't prepared for numbers on a piece of paper, we sure weren't prepared for the news or the pictures on the ultra-sound screen. As it turns out, I had four viewable tumors in my left breast and one tumor in my right breast.

We started discussing options and next steps. We had few options; however, we could have a biopsy, a lumpectomy, chemo, and radiation. *Honey Doc* told me she would give me two months; I had that amount of time to get as many second opinions as I wanted, do my own research, and then get my butt back in her office so she could take care of me however I decided to go forward and battle this enemy.

When I asked her why only two months she said, "Because at the rate these tumors have grown in only a month and a half, we don't have a lot of time to mess around. You don't realize how lucky you are to be here right now – if you had not taken the BRCAnalysis Test, you wouldn't have been sitting in my office. We wouldn't have found these tumors until next year at your next mammogram. Because of your BRCA-1 results and the rate they have grown, it would have been too late to have saved you."

These words hit me like a freight train and I was barely able to breathe. Showing how hard this news was to me, I asked one of the most important questions in my life, knowing that the answer will change me forever, "what would you do if it was your breasts, or a woman in your own family?"

*Honey Doc* told me without a moment's hesitation, "I would have myself or them on an operating table first thing tomorrow morning."

*Honey Doc* wasn't suggesting a lumpectomy, chemotherapy or radiation; she was flat out telling me I needed to have both my breasts cut off to save my life. In medical terminology, it's called a Bilateral (double) Mastectomy. If she was willing to lay down and cut off her own breasts in my shoes, or treat a woman in her own family in the way she was telling me I needed to be treated in order to survive, then enough said.

When I slowed my own tears down enough to see her face, I realized she had tears streaming down as we did. My *Studly* and I knew at that very moment we had one helluva' Oncologist on our side, and she was shooting us straight. The cancer didn't wait ten or so years, it was here now, and we had to be more aggressive in dealing with it than it was with me!

The first person I called with this news was another Oncologist in my cell phone's speed dial (remember, I told y'all we had a profound amount of cancer in my family – and if I'm lying then I'm dying – I gave that man a ring, pronto!) I told his receptionist who I was, who my family was, and what the situation was. By the time she was through taking my information, she was speechless and promised as soon as the doctor was out of the current exam room she would be waiting for him in the hallway.

Within about two hours, the second family oncologist called me at home and told me to run into his office the next morning and he'd see me in between other patients. When my *Studly* and I walked in to see him the next morning, he had a file ready and waiting. *I Love My OB-GYN All to Pieces* and *Honey Doc* had faxed him over every stitch of information they had, and he was ready to talk to us.

The first thing he said was that he'd reviewed the information, but wanted to hear me tell 'my side' of the situation, because he wanted to see just how much we knew and understood about the whole process up to this point. I took a deep breath, ran through it all, and sat back to wait for his response.

He told us both we were very well versed in the issue, we knew the facts, so all that was left of him was to give us his 'what would he do if I was his wife or daughter' opinion. He didn't hesitate one iota – he told me to have the Bilateral Mastectomy, and not wait too much longer.

At this point, my *Studly* and I actually felt a little reassured to tell you the truth! At least not one, not two, but three specialists gave us the exact same answer, which meant they all knew what they were dealing with and they were all on the same page. This particular Oncologists' word in my family was Gospel in a way, meaning if he said it – it was the Gospel Truth! The only reason he wasn't my Primary Oncologist was he specialized in 'different regions' of the body and not the breast; however, he helped both of my grandparents through multiple cancers for over ten years. I knew him, and I trusted his word. Period-Paragraph-End!!!

*Gospel Doc* hugged my neck, told me good luck, and that if I wanted him in my operating room then he'd be there no questions asked.

Right now, we knew we had already received more help, advice, care, and love than most patients ever received. We knew we were so very Blessed. Moreover, we knew what we had to do, and what our decision should be. I still made one more medical call – through the grapevine, I knew of a specialist in New York. This Oncologist specialized in hereditary cancers and alternative medicines or treatments. He also received a copy of my medical file, ultra-sound pictures, and mammogram x-rays. My insurance would have flown us up to New York for a day to visit with this specialist; however, he told me after learning of the issue he'd simply look everything over and call us back at no charge. When our phone rang, *New York, New York* was on the same page as the other doctors – suck it up and do the surgery or risk severe consequences, if not death in the long run.

Now remember, this man was a specialist in alternative medicines and he still told us to move forward with a traditional mastectomy! That was it; we had all the answers we needed to satisfy us and it had been less than a week and a half.

The next morning, I called *Honey Doc* and let her know we agreed, but had a ton of questions regarding who, what, when, where, and how categories. Within a few days, we were back in her office, legal pad full of questions to ask, and spaces in between those lines where we could write the answers down....we were ready for business. It took less than an hour for her to explain to us that because of the situation, location of the lumps, and family history she wanted to do a Bilateral Mastectomy, meaning she was going to take both of my breasts and not just one.

Damn!!!

*Honey Doc* explained the different types of mastectomy surgeries; how the surgeon's can remove the breast and let the tissue heal before opening it back up to install an expander implant, staying flat for the rest of your life and never even choosing to go through reconstructive surgery, and so on. All I could think about was the fact that I'm twenty-eight years old, and you're dang right I want my boobs back! I realized just how personal this decision was, and how each woman chooses differently based on her own wants and needs; however, I wanted my boobs back. And quite frankly, if I'm about to do this, then whomever the reconstructive surgeon is better make it worth my while.

She only trusted one particular reconstructive surgeon and she assured us that if it was her butt lying on the table there would be only one man touching her skin and she was dead serious. They were not in cahoots with one another's medical practice; he was just that good and they made 'pretty new boobs' together! We consulted over the phone with the last two specialists I mentioned as well, and they were astounded to learn 'he' would be handling the reconstruction after the double mastectomy and even reassured me I didn't have the best in Atlanta – I had the best in the Southeastern Region. OK, so let's go meet this *Super Doc* and see what he has to say.

Before walking into the Reconstructive Surgeon's office, I had a day or two of phone calls notifying a specific few people. I called my parents and caught them up on the situation thus far, answering every question I could, writing down other's to ask at the next visit, and trying so very hard to be rational and logical. I knew I needed to be brave and keep my emotions as out of it as best as I could, because I can get pretty flippin' emotional y'all, even though I usually give a tough image! I might be a grown woman, but I knew if I went into a conversation upset with my parents that neither one of my them would take me serious, they'd think I was over-reacting to some x-ray glitch if you know what I mean.

I also called my insurance and benefit coordinator at work to tell her what had transpired and get her advice as to how to handle the issue with deductibles, payments, insurance companies, the whole sha-bang.

When we finally walked into meet *Super Doc*, we were more prepared for discussion than ever before, and apparently it showed by the accordion file, and the stern looks on our faces. We were ushered into his comfy lil' consulting room equipped with soft love seats, easy chairs, and a picnic basket beside 'his' chair.

*Hmmm....wonder what in the heck's in that picnic basket?*

Just as I was about to be nosy, in walks *Super Doc.* My first impression of his white coat, stylish cuff links, and nifty little office was 'this man's young enough to understand where we're coming from, but experienced enough to command the respect of surgeon's much older than he is' sort of feeling. Then he told us first things first, we had the rest of his afternoon and all night long if that's what we needed.

Excuse me? The rest of your afternoon? Don't you mean we have about an hour or so tops and anything else we leave with your receptionist?

No ma'am, I'm yours until you're satisfied you're making the right decision and you're comfortable knowing that I will take care of you as if you were my own family.

Double damn!!!

Here came the tears again, and I just sat there spilling my guts about the whole scary as hell situation, ending with me confessing to this man that I was just about to be too nosey and peek in that picnic basket of his. Bless his heart, he sat there just listening to my *Studly* and I, as we blubbered on, all the while just handing us more and more Kleenex.

When we were through, he took a deep breath, and let us know that we had options on the reconstruction end of the deal. We could either cut off all of the breast mound skin itself leaving me flat as a flitter, then stretch the skin and muscles out very slowly, we could do a skin-saving mastectomy and immediately install expander implants or we could simply wait and do the reconstruction later. It was up to us; he gave us plenty of information packets on each option and let us know we didn't have to make a decision right this very minute if we didn't want to. What I wasn't prepared for was what came outta *Super Doc's* mouth next; he asked me,

"If you could wave your magic wand and make this situation all better then what would you do?"

Do what? That certainly wasn't a question I'd thought about! *Studly* and I looked surprisingly at each other, noodled over ideas for a second, and here I went – I told him if I got a hold of that magic wand then I'd want to wake up from this surgery and have at least something on my chest resembling breast mounds, despite the fact I'd bitched and complained for years about my cup size (my family teased me since the age of 14 that I had to use rebar instead of underwire in my cups) I would want to get back to being myself as soon as I possibly could even if it meant unnecessary pain, and I didn't want him to mess with my tattoo running from my rib cage down my hip and onto my thigh if he didn't have to. That thing cost me a ton of money, five and a half hours of pain, six weeks of healing, and made me feel sexier than a pin-up poster of Sophia Loren.

*Super Doc's* jaw dropped wide open, and he busted out laughing so hard I thought he'd wet his own britches! He just looked over at my *Studly* shaking his head, while my *Studly* looked right back grinning from ear to ear, and told him that attitude was one of the reasons why he loved me so much and married me in the first place. *Super Doc* took a deep breath, snickered once more, looked me square in the eye and told me,

"That won't be a problem!"

Now, in my past when I heard women speak of what they could and could not do without in the events of emergencies, I would always just shake my head in disbelief. Now that an emergency was upon me, I realized I just wanted to be ME when this was all over with. My tattoo is a huge part of me in every aspect of the way, as much a part of me as my large breasts. I just wanted to be me again, and I would never judge another person's personal decision again.

*Super Doc* went on to inform us how the entire procedure would go, and that he would wind up being the primary doctor after the first surgery.

Yup – it was going to take quite a few surgeries but he guaranteed me that when it was all said and done I'd be extremely pleased with my new set of boobs.

To begin with, he would be in the operating room with *Honey Doc* from the very beginning. He would assist *Honey Doc* during the double mastectomy, then when it was his turn she would still be there assisting him. The entire operation would take up to 10 hrs with no complications, up to 12 hours if there were complications. Hmmm, well at least I'd finally get some good sleep!

*Super Doc* would do all the measuring and drawing out where to cut and not cut so to speak. Even better at this point, the only visible scars I would have would be on my back and not anywhere on my breasts. Now folks, this part is really cool – *Super Doc* has learned over the past years how to go about not creating scars unless absolutely necessary, after all he is a plastic surgeon. *Honey Doc* was going to remove my nipples because they have ducts behind them where cancer can hide, leaving an open circle on my breasts.

Second, he is going to use a pumpkin carving scoop and hull out the breast organs, nerves, muscles and any other cool stuff that needs to come out to get rid of the ol' cancer cells. Third, he'll cut back the breast tissue that used to be my boobs, take skin flaps from my back in the shape of circles, and use the flaps to replace where my nipples used to be. Later on, these flaps would become my nipples through nipple reconstruction. However, for now, the only scars visible would be a circle of stitches reconnecting what breast tissue I had left to the circle skin flaps.

Once the nipple reconstruction was complete on down the road, *Super Doc* would tattoo on the color (more tats – how cool is that??) which would totally hide those front scars. Awesome, huh? During the back part of the surgery, *Super Doc* would literally cut two crescent shaped patterns near my shoulder blades so that he could disconnect the third latisimus dorsi muscle from my spine, stretch it over itself past my ribs and reconnect it to the front of my sternum. This had to happen because

I had four muscles on either side of the back of my rib cage and could afford to give one up to the boobs, they were going to have to have some sort of support system.

The rebar in my former bras was not going to do the trick. Therefore, the back scars would be it as far as anything major goes – I can handle that! Scars give character any way and I have enough of them already so what would a few more matter. Besides, I'd have fun telling friends I got them in a bar fight somewhere and telling the kids they came from the Saber Tooth Tiger that jumped out at me. So no biggie.

When I woke up from surgery, *Super Doc* said I'd be bandaged up like a mummy and would have four drain tubes coming out of me – two from my sides close to my rib cage, and two from my back below my shoulder blades. The drain tubes would allow the excess fluids and gunk to flow away from the implants and incessions. I would recover in the hospital for a minimum of three days, being waited on hand and foot by his best nurses, they would teach us both the proper care and handling of the drain tubes, and when it was time for me to go home I would go feeling as well as could be expected.

Each week after that, I would be chauffeured to his office where I would receive my 'fill-ups' from either him or his *Lovely Assistant*, and yes ma'am – she was as good as he was at it and she was his wingman. When the fill-ups had me back at the size I was at before they lopped off my original boobs, then he'd let me rest for about four weeks so the elasticity settled and then he would perform the second surgery. *Super Doc* would remove the expander implants and install my permanent implants. After that I would have anywhere between four to six weeks to heal up and we would begin the nipple reconstruction. My nipples had to be removed regardless of which style of surgery we elected to have because the inside of the nipple has ducts, which allow cancer to hide in.

Fine – take 'em too, while you're at it. After the nipple reconstruction surgery would come the final procedure – just a procedure, not a surgery. They would tattoo on my nipples. Holy Hell, I've heard of a lot of different kinds of tattoos, cosmetic and otherwise, even heard of people who tattoo their privates; however, I'd never heard of a tattooed nipple! *Super Doc* told us he had a cosmetic tattoo artist on his staff and she specialized in medical-plastic-surgeon-cosmetic sort of tattoos and she even had a book I could look at of before and after photographs. By the way, you get to pick out what color and size you want your nipples to be. Sure thing, put me down for a sexy dusky rose – pointed up just enough to catch my *Studly's* eye – and about half the size they are right now, thank y'all very much! Hey – for anyone trying to fit into a pretty little bikini top – nipple size matters.

When we finished with our Pow-Wow session, my *Studly* and I just looked over at each other from our perches on the soft loveseat in that cozy lil' consultation room, we both grinned from ear to ear, and literally felt all our fears and worries melting away off our shoulders. No wonder all these other top notch surgeons were so excited about us heading to see *Super Doc*. He gave us peace.

# Let's Get It On
## *Feeling unprepared for battle – going in anyway*

Now remember when I told y'all I had only talked with my parents up until this point. I did that for a reason. I'm the type of person who wants all their ducks in a row before I open my trap and spill the beans in public. I even put the burden on my parents by asking them to NOT talk to anyone in our family or friends until we'd gotten it all figured out. It was my body, and when I wanted to talk to people about my boobs being cut off then I would. It was no one else's place, but mine! My parents raised me, they know how I am, and they were respectful about my wish. (But they sure as heck were burning up the phone wires talking with each other!) Besides, we've had way too much cancer in our family to start second, third, and twelveth hand gossip. When people heard, it needed to come straight from the source.

That's why when I went to tell my Nana (whom by the way at this time is a six year breast cancer survivor herself) I took my *Studly* and my Mama along, and even made sure my granddaddy would be there, too. It was time to confess what I'd been diagnosed with and hiding over the past few weeks. We all walked into the kitchen where my Nana was halfway through fixing dinner, and watched her face fall then guard over because she knew something was wrong by the way we walked in her back door.

She slammed down her wooden spoon, covered the pots on the stove, turned off the burners, placed her hands on those sassy lil' hips, and said, "Go ahead and shoot."

I took a deep breath and said, "The punch line is I've got breast cancer, and I'm going in for a double mastectomy and reconstruction."

You would've thought a ton of bricks had been dropped on her shoulders, and in a sense, they had. I watched her face as year's worth of anxiety, surgeries, complications, chemo and radiation flashed so hard and heavy it could be felt across the room. She went to boo-hooing, and it was all I could do to suck in my own fears so I could be strong for her. I assured her this had been caught as early as it possibly could have, pulled up a chair and told her the whole story that led us to her kitchen table, and that I WAS going to come through this with flying colors...specifically, a dusky rose color which would be my new nipples and by the way those nipples were going to be attached to the best looking set of perky boobs in our whole family!

She and my granddaddy fell out laughing through their tears, and said the good news is my boobs would never be in a race to see which got to my belly button first. I just love my grandparents all to pieces, too.

The next person I called was my Aunt. Now I know all y'all have that one crazy Aunt you know you can go to with whatever ails you. The kind of Aunt that has been there, done that, got the t-shirt, and then tie-dyed it. She's lived her life hard enough and long enough to not take any crap off anybody, can dish it out as good as she can take it, and still comes back for more. Well guess what? I guarantee you my aunt can beat up yours!

She listened carefully as I told it all, and then told me I was a sissy for not telling her to her face because we both knew she would've punched me right between the eyes for not including her in on this party from the beginning. Then she also told me that if she were in the same position and knew all the same facts, that she would do the surgery, too. When I did get to see her a few days later she didn't punch me as I thought she would. She didn't even wrestle me to the ground as she has in the past. She just opened her arms wide and loved me like only she can. I am one lucky, spoiled-rotten brat. And I know it, too!

You know, telling people you have sumthin' wrong with you takes guts, I don't care who you are. We are very blessed in our life, because we have something very few people have. We have true blue – all out – honest to goodness friends. We all go out every single Tuesday night for hot wings and beer, and we even have our 'regular' restaurants we go to because they're big enough and experienced enough to handle all of us. There could be only a dozen of us or all three dozen of us might show up. Doesn't matter really, because whoever shows up shows up and nobody gets their panties in a wad if someone isn't there - most of the time. However, it was time to tell the gang and I imagined that would be worse than all the rest.

There isn't anything we haven't dealt with in our circle of friends and I do mean anything – we've had crazy ex-spouses that needed to be taken out behind the shed and the sense beat into them, we've had financial worries, moving parties, other surgeries, addictions, and bon fires to sometimes get rid of the evidence. Nevertheless, I was the baby of the group, and nothing like this is supposed to happen to someone so young. I thought in my trying-to-be-logical mind that we needed to just invite the whole gang over to our house that Tuesday night and we'd drop the bomb all at one time. Trouble is, we knew not everyone would show up so I was still going to have to repeat this story a few more times but what the heck, it was worth a try.

The funny thing is, the Monday afternoon before we were to all go out and eat I got a phone call at my desk at work and as soon as I picked it up off the receiver, I could hear a friend blessing me up one side and down the other, and lemme' just tell you –it wasn't that kind of blessing. I let her rant and rave and just waited quietly for her to finish. I certainly understood her frustration. Then when it was my turn to speak, I told her the facts and apologized for not coming to her sooner but that I wanted to get my facts straight before going public with my cancer for so many obvious reasons.

She pouted for a while, but still told me she loved me and supported my decision. "And oh by the way, the whole gang has heard the gossip about you already so you might as well clear the air by sending out an email you big dummy." Leave it up to a true friend to tell it like it is and think of the quickest way to get the word out.

Last but not least, I had to inform my boss and teammates at work about the situation. I had to figure out how I went about the medical leave of absence, train someone to fill my shoes or try to while I was out for about 12 weeks of work, and make a game plan of what to do when I returned. I bet y'all have figured out by now I'm an organization and communications freak! I just wanted to make sure my guys at work were taken care of, cause lil' Mama would be out of it for a while. It was easier than I thought it would be, guys don't like hearing all the gory girlie private details, and they don't run their mouths in my dept like others in the office do. They kept it as quiet as they could, informed people on a need to know basis, and anyone that didn't know would find out soon enough when the temp was there sitting behind my desk. Fair enough.

The week before my double mastectomy, I received two very special gifts from family & friends. Prayer Shawls. My husband and I bought our cabin less than two miles from a man I work with and his wife, never even knowing we were so close together on opposite sides of the mountain. We had all planned on going out to lunch one day, and when they walked in with a gift bag I thought *Please, Lord – let me hold myself together and not start boo-hooing over something sentimental.* We got through lunch and I explained what all the doctors had informed me was going to happen the next Monday morning. You know – small talk of chopping off the boobs, tossing them away, inserting flat water balloons, major stitches, etc. before our lunch was served. By the time soup and salad was served, they both were stunned and ghost white! Studly and I were so used to the story by now, we couldn't help but secretly grin and pretend to carry on like the dinner table conversation was no big deal!

Once we were through eating and chatting, the gift bag was handed over. I tried being as polite as possible, and even joked that I didn't know pre-surgical gifts were all the rage now. But when I crumpled up the tissue paper sticking out of the gift bag, what was inside stunned me into silence. Grace leaned over and helped me by holding onto one of my hands, and pulling out the prettiest little quilted shawl I'd ever seen. The colors were absolutely beautiful, and it looked and felt so cozy as she just wrapped me up in it in the middle of the restaurant. Also in the bag, were several sheets of paper printed out from a computer. The papers told the story of the prayer shawl, how it came to be, and how each shawl was made by a Sunday School Class. Even the colors of the fabric had special meaning. Each shawl was constructed with specific healing powers and thoughts prayed over it while the Sunday School members worked on it tirelessly from beginning to end. Well, that was it – here came the water works and they splashed all over that new quilted shawl. That was quite alright though they both said, it was ultra tear absorbent and would see me through every surgery. When it came time to pack the suitcase for our tropical hospital getaway, the prayer shawl went into my small carry-on. It wasn't leaving my side.

The second prayer shawl was crocheted, with the softest yarn that I just wanted to bury my face in. The color of the yarn was chosen with care from my Aunt's Sunday School Class, and had been prayed over as well during the crocheting. Now this shawl just happened to be delivered the day before my favorite Sunflower was coming home for a visit. She took one look at this 'new pretty' and tossed it over her shoulder like a beauty queen, prancing around playing dress up! Turns out that prayer shawls aren't just for patients, they are sent to provide comfort and snuggles to the family & friends, too.

Scheduling the surgery wound up being quite a circus trick! I thought all that was involved was simply a doctor, calling a hospital, and Ta-Da it was done. No, no. It took *Super Doc's Amazing Admin, Honey Doc's* crew, the hospital surgery scheduler, and me to make this happen. I know they wished I hadn't been involved, but at the time it seemed to me like the right thing to do after I was told my surgery would happen on this day, no wait the next week out, the following month out, and I finally put my foot down.

Listen, when you're told you have something wrong with you on the inside – it's all you can think about. Remember that scene in *The Mummy* with Brendan Frasier where the Egyptian prison guard becomes the guide and the Scarab Beetle begins crawling under his skin? That was what happened to me in my mind. I began to feel as if spots of cancer were crawling inside of me and by God, I wanted them out! The longer they put my surgery off, the worse the heebie-jeebies got. No joke. You tell me I have cancer and you're going to help me by removing it, but then schedule and reschedule me three to four times. I'm freaking out over here, HELLO!

Well, guess what? There is a waiting room full of other cancer patients with the heebie-jeebies in front of you, and they're waiting to get into the OR, too! Calm down, drink some warm milk if you have to, but realize you are not the only patient on the roster for surgery, and if it were actually a life or death situation your team of doctors would've had you on the table before you even knew what was happening. You'll be fine, you're in good hands, now let the good team of doctors get you in at the first available time and be patient if a true emergency comes along and pushes you out of the way. It's most likely going to happen to matter how big or small the hospital is, so suck it up and deal with it!

# Double Mastectomy
## *Morphine is My Friend*

The weekend before my surgery, I had two things on my agenda: partying and shopping! Mama and I put our heads together about things like getting the house deep cleaned, button-front pajama's for the hospital stay that would give the doctors easy access, overnight bags for the hospital stay for my *Studly* and I, and getting our nails done. It's just a necessity at times, go with me on this last one y'all.

Friday and Saturday mornings, I scrubbed our home from top to bottom, and got all the cracks in between. I knew Mama, other family members and friends would dearly love me to ask them for help while I was recovering at home – but some things are deeply personal and for me cleaning is one of them. No one can clean your house like you can (and if they can, you better take a good long look at yo' self in the mirror!) Around brunch time, Mama swung by the house and picked me up so we could go shop – we were on a mission: button front pj's and they had to look somewhat pretty as much for the hospital stay as for me.

Let me tell you something, button front pj's are just about unheard of apparently, because we looked for hours finally finding something that didn't resemble frumpiness and that were soft as a baby's bottom. I got five pair knowing that I would need them – trust me when I say this:

you are going to sweat at night AND during the day from struggling with illness, you're going to be sore as hell from surgery and won't be able to pull anything over your head for about a month and a half minimum, and your bandages & drain tubes are going to stain the inside of those pj's and you don't want company coming over to see that. It's the truth, so realize it and deal with it.

After I forked over money for the pj's, we headed to the nail salon. The doctor's and the pre-op nurses let me know that I could not have on nail polish for the surgery....riiiiiight....so I walked into the salon and asked for a French manicure and pedicure. I might be having my boobs cut off, but I'm not about to look down the hospital bed and not see SOMETHING pretty! Even the nail salon technicians and owner heard about my surgery, and they promised to come to the house and repolish whenever I needed them to if I couldn't get out or didn't feel like it. You know, sometimes it pays off when small towns gossip.

Saturday afternoon and evening, a friend of our group was throwing one helluva' pool party! We headed over there about two pm and didn't leave until after midnight – we didn't go over there with swimsuits on either; we just brought the biggest cooler in the garage. And that's all I've got to say about that!

Monday morning of my surgery sure did roll around quick. I didn't sleep at all the night before even though I knew I was firm and comfortable with the decision I had made, so when the alarm went off at four thirty a.m. I was wide-awake and ready to slap that button. We had bags packed already, clothes laid out on the footboard of the bed, and damn it I couldn't even have a cup of coffee. Great. You know you aren't supposed to have anything to eat or drink past midnight before your surgery....so the night before I put my beer down at 11:59:59! There are times you simply have the right to drink if you so choose: when you're eighteen and old enough to go into battle for your country, and the night before your boobs are going to be cut off are two prime examples.

# Blue Tattoos

We marched ourselves into one side of the hospital, while my family marched into another, and within just a few minutes in walked *Super Doc.* I was ready in my sexy white support hose stockings, open front hospital gown, and no make-up – lemme just tell ya! He pulled out a blue sharpie marker and told me to come on over, it was time for my blue tattoos as he affectionately called them. He marked me up like a connect-the-dots coloring book, then stood back to admire his handy work. Feeling very sure and pleased with himself, he shook my *Studly's* hand once again and gave me a squeeze and told me I had a few minutes before they wheeled me into surgery so I better talk to my family right quick so they wouldn't worry about me so much.

I got to see them one at time for a few seconds a piece and kept my happy face on cracking jokes and lewd comments about myself to keep them all smiling and laughing. When the pre-op nurses kicked the foot brakes of my hospital bed off and wheeled me out towards the surgical wing, my *Studly* and my Nana were holding my hands across the bed rails walking with me. I knew they were in on this journey with me, but it's just a little image like that makes all the difference to me in the world.

I had a slew of nurses coming at me, one takes your blood pressure, one sticks you with all the IV needles, one checks your support hose to make sure you aren't cheating by taking them off, and every single one of them ask you for legalities sake if you know what you're in the hospital for. Now I had quite a few smart-alleck comments to make, but I was a good girl and kept the smirks off my face when I told them all yes ma'am and sir, I'm here for a Bilateral Mastectomy, I'm BRCA-1 positive, and when this is all over with I'm going to be perky for the rest of my life!

*Honey Doc* also came into see me, we went thru her steps and processes just like *Super Doc* had gone through his while marking me up, she told me she admired and respected me for doing the right thing, then gave me a wink and I'd see her when I woke up later on tonight.

Last but not least, *Mama Anesthesia* came to tell me she would be with me for the entire surgery – no potty breaks, no meals, no nothing – she was mine and I was her and that was all there was to it for better or worse. Welllll….speaking of worse, it suddenly dawned on me that years ago during Appendicitis, I made a total fool of myself coming out of anesthesia and regret to this day what I said out loud….that stuff that costs about $11,000.00 on your itemized medical bill is a truth serum and it was out to get me – I just knew it. Therefore, I confessed to *Mama Anesthesia* and my *Studly*, that I did NOT want anyone in the post-op recovery room with me other than him. He knew about my last blunder , I gave him fair warning that things might fly out of my mouth I would never in a million years say or even think under normal circumstances, and he promised he'd let it go in one ear and out the other if I even said anything at all. It was more than I could ask for from anyone else, so I accepted his offer to stand by me no matter what top-secret-skeletons I might reveal and then he leaned down and gave me the sweetest, wettest, warmest kiss I have ever been blessed with. When we both opened our eyes and found the other staring back already we just smiled and he whispered, "Night-night, baby…."

The last thing I remember was *Mama Anesthesia* helping me slide off my hospital bed and onto a flat, tiny operating table on some sort of white pedestal with the light shining down on me. Yup, I felt like I was laying myself down for the sacrifice. Good thing she hit my IV with the go-go juice and asked me to count backwards from 10. Funny thing is I don't remember even gearing up my brain to think anymore at all.

# I gave all y'all warning...

Then it was time to wake up. I literally remember feeling myself wake up mad as a wet hen, and voila – that truth serum decided to rear up its ugly head and lash out. Wanna know why? Because when I opened my eyes, both *Honey Doc* and *Super Doc* were standing over me along with an entourage of nurses scurrying about, and every single family member was cluttering up that big hospital room making it feel absolutely tiny. Oh yeah, and not to mention I was sideways in the bed, hurting like hell, couldn't move at all, my IVs in my right arm were pulling and tangled up in the bed rail, I had an E.T.Phone Home red finger on my left hand trying to phone home, and my legs were trapped and compressing because of calf style blood pressure cuffs. FAB-A-LUS!

Ready or not, here I came….I began hollering at the doctors and nurses letting them know they could get these $%^&* cuffs off my legs, if they couldn't untangle the %$& IVs from the dang-blasted bed rail then I'd do it myself! I glared at the head nurse when she tried to come over and press me back into the bed, shot her the bird with my left hand telling her where she could stick the E.T. red finger thingy and flicking it off my left hand after several tries, and oh yeah – why in the @#$% were all my family members in my room? That was all it took, I heard my Mama across the room say 'we're outta here' and she grabbed my best girlfriend by the arm, blocked Nana from getting any closer into the room, looked over at my stepmama and used a tone that meant business and they all scattered like they'd just witnessed a scene from The Exorcist first hand!

The only ones left in the room were my *Studly* and my Daddy. He lasted about five minutes according to the doctors and my *Studly*, and then my tough-as-nails Daddy even fled the room. Can't blame him for that – no parent wants to witness their child become a demon.

Next thing I remember is *Super Doc* taking a horse syringe to my IV line, and injecting yet another clear liquid I like to call the 'calm yourself down or I'll do it for you' juice. I heard a few snide snickers coming from all around the room, then *Super Doc* and my *Studly* re-situated me in bed and fixed all the lil' issues I so sweetly pointed out before. It wasn't until the next morning that I woke up and looked around to see my *Studly* curled up in his own make shift bed next to me, and I think I saw concern on his face but it wasn't the relief kind of concern it was more like the 'please Lord, give me strength to deal with the demon' kind of concern. I just smiled and slyly asked him if I did alright….he mirrored my sly smile and said, "No worries babe – you did just fine."

Riiiight. Everything I thought I remembered was true and we'd just add a new chapter to the truth serum's and call it Part II.

It was two days after my surgery before *Super Doc* removed the bandages. By now, I was totally in love with my team of morning, noon, and night shift nurses and we were all on good terms and I was back to behaving like a normal human being. Therefore, when all three of them came in with *Super Doc* I was a little surprised because I knew it was shift change time and one had come in extra early. What I didn't know was how rare and unheard of a double mastectomy is for us young BRCA-1 mutants, because the test itself is still so new. The nurses wanted to see my breast mounds and scars, it was as much curiosity as it was for medical lessons learned, so I said not a problem – I'm sure they've seen a lot worse anyways.

I stared up at the ceiling while *Super Doc* removed my mummy wraps and heard gasps all around. But they weren't Oh-My-God kind of gasps; they were Oh-Wow gasps! I took a deep breath and looked down at myself and even I got excited. I had boobs! They were very small, hard as bricks, kaddywhompus, and sort of smooched flat – but they were there just like *Super Doc* promised they would be. It was at this very moment we all realized just how mental this really is – physical pain lasts for a while, but the mental can stick to you like peanut butter on a rib cage. When I looked down and saw that progress had been made already, everything simply fell into place and felt better. I knew things were going to work out just fine, because at this point I had nowhere to go but up.

Speaking of up, it was time for me to get my butt up out of that hospital bed and say hello to the world. Ok, the hallways at least and maybe another patient if there were any on the same floor. Off we trotted into the hallway equipped with pj's, slip on pink tennis shoes, robes, drain tubes and an IV tower to conquer and divide. Yeah, the conquering was when I walked from the bed to the hospital room door – it kicked my butt, I won't lie.

The drain tubes pulled at my back even though my team of nurses had safety pinned the four of them underneath my pajama top (which was by the way ingenious, because if they hadn't I would have been walking around holding the little pouches that are connected to the end of the drain tubes that look like grenades. No kidding, I looked like I was packing explosives under my clothes.) The IV had my arm and hand sore as heck, one foot was dragging sideways like it was about to fall off, I couldn't see a dadgum thing because my eye sight was all blurry, and by the way I had to make at least three laps on my first attempt walking from the door to the nurses' station about 25 feet away. Riiiiight.

The dividing part came next, because I was frustrated at my limbs and eyesight. I went in for my boobs; what the heck had they done to my foot and my eyes? Turns out, *Mama Anesthesia* packs a whollop! Between that and the painkillers, my eyesight was shot-out and my foot was asleep on the end of my leg for well over twenty-four hours! All I wanted to do was walk the frigging laps and get back to my bed, so I took off like a bat out of hell dividing myself from my *Studly* and visitors and there I went. Straight to the handicap rail mounted to the sidewall of the hallway.

Here came my *Studly* to save me from myself quite frankly, and it was a good thing he did because about that time I realized the morphine pump began to beep letting me know it was ok for me to have a shot. I grabbed that trigger and hit that button so many times I thought my thumb would fall off, and he just kept laughing at me saying it was alright and I could push that lil' trigger all I wanted to. After all, it only dispenses the amount of juice *Super Doc* would allow it to and even then only once every eight minutes.

Which reminded me, I believed I needed to talk to *Super Doc* about the timing mechanism of my pump because ... well, just because I needed it more than a shot every eight minutes and unless he wanted to deal with the demon again I would politely suggest he grant my request or else I would just have to bless his lil' heart. It all sounded perfectly logical to me, and I was sure he would understand. Oh no wait, he couldn't – his boobs hadn't been cut off – so he'd just have to work with me on it.

By the time I had made one lap and rested every few feet in between; I actually had a little wind in my sail and wanted to try for another. Turns out I could walk even though body parts weren't exactly cooperating and the next thing I knew I passed the test and was allowed to lay back down in the bed. Oh good, just in time for the next CSI episode! Hmmm....that walking thing wasn't as bad as I thought it would be. Maybe next time I had to go potty, I'd walk another lap just to see if I could. The challenge was on!

It suddenly dawned on me that it was Wednesday. My surgery was on Monday morning. Good Lord, what was that smell? Surely to goodness, something had crawled into my bed and died while I was out walking the halls. That smell can't possibly be coming from me. OH-MY-GOD, it is!

Why in the world nobody tells you that after a surgery and lying in a hospital bed that won't quit inflating every time you try to resituate yourself, you are flat out rank! I barked out an order to shut the hospital room door, throw the curtain, and strip me down naked as a jay bird – I had to wash. Now thankfully, I had packed our brand of soap and we had an unused bedpan just beckoning for someone to run some hot water into it. Spit bath, here I come! My sweet *Studly* got me a nice pot of bedpan water and a washrag with some soap on it and handed it over. I just looked at him. What in the world, was I supposed to do with this? I could hardly move my arms. After we discussed our options of staying in the bed or standing back up again and taking the lesser of two evils, he wrinkled up his nose and gently went to work. God, I love this man. He scrubbed me from forehead down to my pinky toes getting all the cracks in between. This was better than Mama's 409 – and it can take the rust off a bumper! There is just nothing like feeling clean and refreshed when you really need it. And you really need to get that surgery stink off you!

Early that same evening, *Super Doc* sent in Head Nurse with an order for me to receive two Ambien – those wonder drug sleeping pills everyone is talking about. I'd never needed sleeping pills before and I really didn't think I needed them now, so I politely let her know I would rather not thank y'all very kindly, and thought that would be the end of it. Oh no, uh-uh, *Super Doc* had spoken, Head Nurse was on a mission, and they knew I needed one good night of rest finally before they would send me home tomorrow. Fine. I took my lil' plastic medicine cup, sipped from my hospital water jug, and thought what the heck – if nothing else maybe I would finally get some sleep. Y'all know how hospitals are, they're just doing their jobs but they come into your room every hour on the hour taking blood pressure, temperatures, and asking you questions like, "Why aren't you sleeping?" Gotta luv it!

About two hours and bed checks later, Head Nurse couldn't believe I still had my eyes open staring up at the TV screen. I felt like my eyes couldn't close if my life depended on it. I could literally feel my whole body tense and the nerves fraying more and more every second because of what those two Ambien did to my system. I was wired for sound and sarcastic as hell about it, too. Some people can be drowsy when the medicine says it will make them that way, and others of us have to be trouble makers and have opposite reactions to every flippin' thing. I was just watching the minutes tick by on the clock, waiting for *Super Doc* to waltz in so I could give him what for. Each time Head Nurse poked her head in the door to peek at me, I was peeking right back just waving and inviting her on in to watch reruns of CSI with me. But we were the only one's awake that night…my *Studly* was sawing logs on the make shift couch in my room, all snuggled down deep in extra hospital blankets and bed sheets. Bless his heart, I just wanted to scream at everyone involved that night but thought twice about it and saved my energy.

The next morning rolled around and sleeping beauty woke up from his good night's sleep…by now I'm thinking it was a conspiracy and I got placebos while he got the good drugs. Guess who trots on into my room daring to look all chipper and smile at me? One guess, come on… Yup, *Super Doc*. He got about three steps into the room saying, "Good Mor…" and stopped dead in his tracks when he saw the look on my face! His eyes got big as saucers and goes Uh-Oh, as if he knew I was about to let him have it.

Y'all this man saved my life and treated me like I was family, I knew I could think dark thoughts but really shouldn't be saying them out loud to him so I decided to take a deep breath and sweetly let him know his sleeping pills didn't exactly do the trick last night. I think it scared him more that I went from fire shooting out of my eye sockets to hearing sappy sweet and calm words coming out of my mouth. He promised he'd never give them to me again and even promised to ask his future patients IF they wanted a little something extra to help them sleep. Mission: Accomplished.

# There's No Place Like Home

When it was time to pack up and head out we were ready. My *Studly* rounded up hospital carts for all my flower arrangements and balloon clusters, and trucked them down two at a time to load up the back of our SUV. It took four carts. Head Nurse helped me put on the same pair of little cotton shorts and slip into the soft zip up sweatshirt I had worn into pre-op just a few days ago. *Studly* got back to our room, tossed the toiletries and pj's into the small overnight bag, and we were off. Wait – I couldn't walk out of the hospital, I had to ride in a wheel chair from my room to the elevator, through the lobby, and out the front sliding doors. Fantastic. This whole time all I heard was walk-walk-walk, and now they wanted me to ride. Whatever. Just grit your teeth and do what you're told, because at this point all my modesty had flown the coop.

We rolled to a stop on the sidewalk, and I stepped as easily as possible into the SUV. Then I realized I'd forgotten my pillow. Screw it, I'd just lean forward for the forty-five minute ride home. Remember now, at this point the drain tubes are left in your sides and back therefore making you as uncomfortable as possible. That's their job, and it's yours to deal with the pain they cause. Good to know. And the ride home is even more fun than the hospital stay: you can go slow and hit all the potholes in the road, or you can speed over them and get home quicker. It's your choice, and not an easy call to make whichever way you decide to go. My advice is pop two pain pills and floor it, you can lean forward and hold onto the Oh-Shit handle with a death grip.

Then came the front steps to the house. Lovely. However, you're almost there and if you can just get your aching tired butt into the front door and sink into your recliner you know everything will just be alright. Surprise! All those flower arrangements that gagged you on the ride home are now being toted into the living room and placed just so-so on the hearth beside you. All your friends and family love you, and sending sick folks in the hospital a flower arrangement is simply the right thing to do. What isn't the right thing to do is send them covered in pollen and not-quite-ready-yet buds that want to wait to open when you're home.

Here came the sneezing fits and I do mean a bunch of 'em. Anyone who has ever had their back kaddywhompus and out of whack knows that sneezing is the last thing you EVER want to happen because it feels like your already kinked muscles and spine will just explode right outta your skin. Try sneezing when you've got two eight scars and stitches running right up under your shoulder blades, four drain tubes stitched into your skin with grenade pouches hanging, muscles you didn't even know you had disconnected and reconnected to your sternum, expanding water jugs inside your chest where your boobs used to be, and two skin flaps that feel like torpedo launchers. When you've been though that, THEN you can come and talk to me about yo' sneezing fits! Good Lord in Heaven, I know you gave me a crystal ball to my breast cancer but if you'd just take me, right now I promise I'll be a good angel, fluff the other angels' feathers, and even wash your chariot every day. Just please don't let me having another sneezing fit. Careful what you ask for....I quit sneezing and my eyes started watering buckets for days. The Lord has such an awesome sense of humor!

OK, so you're finally in your recliner with just the right pillows propped up behind you, and it's now time to simply sink and let them world slip away. Suga', not in my neighborhood! The twilight bark had sounded, and the troops were marching our way. For hours, our front door was constantly rotating with the onslaught of company coming to bring plates and Tupperware containers of food.

That's another thing we do in the South – when you're sick, we bring fried chicken and all the fixins. It's only proper and if we didn't then our ancestors would come up outta the grave and get us! Y'all think we're lying, but it'll happen! So here they came….everyone from every generation of family and friends bringing comfort food (pssst….it's really their prize winning recipes so they can show off to whoever opens the refrigerator door next, so don't let them fool you!)

We had so much food it spilled out of the fridge and onto our counter tops – we literally had so much food we wouldn't possibly be able to eat it all before it ruined. We did the only two things we knew to do: we told everyone that brought food next that if they put one in then they had to take two out, and we called my stepson home from college. By the time Baby Boy finished munching on a welcome home snack, my *Studly* had every piece of leftover plastic container in our house stuffed with comfort food and packed into the trunk of his car. He'd be everyone's new best friend at the dorm rooms!

Here is a little hint on food after surgery: your taste buds will be 'off' because of either anesthesia or medication (especially if the medication happens to be painkillers!) All that delicious food we had even after the fridge was raided several times simply didn't hit the spot. I was either nauseous when I tried to eat, or simply wasn't hungry because the painkillers make everything numb inside and out. All of a sudden, in walks Nana telling me, "Oh, yes you are going to eat," and "don't give me any backtalk, either!"

Turns out that when all else fails in the world, talk to your grandmother. She has a few tricks up her sleeve like the ultimate chicken salad recipe and a sleeve of saltine crackers with your name written all over them to ease an upset tummy and a kiss to make it all better! Nana's chicken salad did the trick, my appetite came back full swing and I could finally take my antibiotics and painkillers with a little food in my belly.

The second day I was home I had one thought on my mind – give me a true shower! My *Studly* and I gathered up what we thought we'd need and headed to the big guest bathroom downstairs. I would be taking up residence down there since I would need helping hands, and it was easier to maneuver in. The first thing I wanted to do was shave my legs! Good gracious, you'd think a wooly mammoth had snuck into my pajama bottoms and it had only been five days since my surgery! We found out it was easier if I sat on the side of the tub and held my grenade pouches while *Studly* soaped up my legs and took charge of the razor. That actually worked out pretty good believe it or not, and he was real careful to keep feeling of my legs to make sure he hadn't missed any stubble… hehehe, the lil' flirt! Since I still couldn't lift my arms up enough at my sides to even skim the underarms with the razor they would simply have to wait. Dang, I should've thought to maybe have my underarms waxed before this surgery. If I would've done that then I wouldn't have pricked myself constantly and aggravated the drain tubes!

Now so far, we'd found three awesome bath products everyone should have coming home from a surgery like this: No Rinse shampoo, a handicap shower chair, and a long handled bath squishy. The No Rinse shampoo is sold mostly a beauty supply places. Just throw a towel around your shoulders while you sit in the recliner and have someone douse your head with this liquid. As soon as your hair is wet with it, you can start scrubbing like normal and it will actually lather up! When you're through having someone scrub your head, all they have to do is take that towel and start drying your hair – lather and all will come right out and leave you squeaky clean. Amazing stuff, isn't it?

The handicap shower chair can be bought at any apothecary shop, home improvement store, and online too, I'm sure! Ours had been in our family for years, passed around from members with broken bones to births. Things like that you just don't get rid of, you save them and share them with others in need. I could sit in the shower and hold my drain pouches in my lap while someone scrubbed me down as often as I felt like, and trust me – some days you feel like a shower, and some days you do good to get out of the recliner for a spit bath. Both are perfectly acceptable and no one needs to tell you otherwise.

The third tool in our little box of tricks was the long handled shower squishy. Folks, when you have no use of your arms you lose a little bit of muscle tone (for me it was about the second week home....) then you fight and you push those stiff muscles even harder to stretch and loosen up. Having the long handled shower squishy let me wash myself! I can sit on my shower chair, and reach places I didn't think I'd ever be able to reach again....then I also found out when my towel fell off the toilet seat or I couldn't reach out far enough to slide the shower curtain then I could use the length of that handle to do it for me. Ingenious, huh?

Within one week of being home, the mail man began bringing bills. I do mean a lot of them. I had planned on receiving whoppers any way, but didn't plan on more than one. The hospital itself sends a bill for your rent in the OR and the hospital room, drugs used, food ordered, etc. all on an itemized piece of paper. The Anesthesiologists send a bill in the amount of their time, supplies, and chemical cocktail. The Reconstructive Surgeon, Oncologist, and surgical assistant send bills for their equal share of your paycheck, too. Insurance will send you a warning statement, showing just how much they take care of per hospital or doctor first. This is when you throw a party, and thank the good Lord that you opted for the bit more expensive plan in the first place, because you might not think you need all that coverage but when you do need it – it comes in handy!

I realized very quickly that my organizational skills were about to be put to use. I had to keep all the bills separate and accounted for, and all in one place to make sure I didn't miss a payment. So I got a three ring binder and divider tabs from my stash of office supplies and slowly went to work. I knew this was only the first of many surgeries, so I got a set of BIG TABS from the local office supply store. Each surgery was going to have its own BIG TAB, and behind each one I would make the standard small tabs for each hospital or doctor. This worked great! Now each time I got a bill, it was three-hole punched and placed exactly where it needed to go. Anytime I wanted to make a payment over the phone or by mail, all I had to do was flip to the particular bill. Another thing I did was make an Excel spreadsheet in the same fashion. Each surgery was listed by row, and each doctor or hospital by column. Once the monthly payments had been made, I documented it on the bill itself and on the Excel spreadsheet for quicker reference.

You may be wondering why I was making monthly payments in the first place. You see it's like this – when your insurance pays ninety percent and you pay ten percent, those percentages will add up. Especially, when your double mastectomy ran a grand total of fifty-four thousand dollars and change! So trust me when I say that between four or five major bills for each surgery you're going to have, you ask the hospital administrator to set up all your bills on either six month or twelve month payment plans. It would be nice to win the lottery and be able to simply write a check for the total amount of each bill per surgery, but hey – this is the real world and you deal with bills when and how you can.

Now as each doctor visit and follow up appointment was made, I took my three ring binder with me. This became the ultimate reference book for not only me, but for the doctors and their staff. Anytime a question was asked about paperwork, finances and billing, lab results, etc. all I had to do was flip open my handy dandy little binder to the page and got out answers. A place for everything, and everything in its place. Call me old fashioned at times, but that statement rings true so very often.

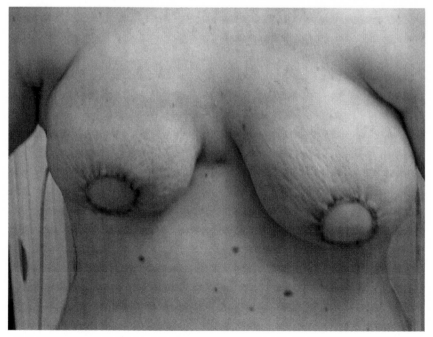

June 25, 2009

First post surgical picture at home. Drain tubes hanging at sides

# Pain-in-the-boob-tubes

The next sore subject you need to know about is these drain tubes... they're a pain in the boob if you know what I mean! Seriously, these drain tubes are no joke. They're extremely uncomfortable and because they come from out of your sides and your back, you can't lay down flat. You'll be sleeping propped way up, or in the recliner. Whichever is most comfortable for you; however, don't confuse real comfort and settling for comfort. Real comfort would be no drain tubes poking you in the tender sides, back or pulling at the stitches holding them in your skin. Yeah, you don't have that luxury yet.

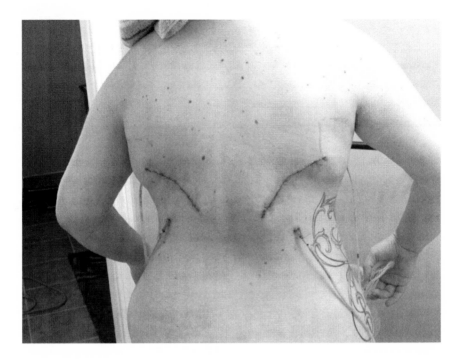

June 25, 2009
Back view of eight inch latisimus dorsi bilateral mastectomy
scars, puckered and puffy from the surgery. Drain tubes
connected in skin by approximately three stitches (right side of
picture shows me holding the drain tube grenade pouches.)

In addition, the doctors will give you homework to complete. It's called
your Drain Chart, and you'll be writing down the amount of liquid
removed from the pouches several times a day or once in the morning
and once before going to bed. This chart is required at every check up you
have at the reconstructive surgeons office, and don't you dare forget it!

The nurses at the hospital will do it for you, and show you how to strip
the tubes and empty the pouches while you gaze in awe. However,
when you get home it will be a test of just how well you paid attention
in class. The tubes are supposed to drain away not only the yellowish
and reddish fluid from around the surgical area, but they will also drain
away fatty tissue (liposuction while you sleep, I like the sound of that
don't you?) You'll hold the tube with one hand as close to the rib cage

and stitches as you can muster, and use your thumbnail and first finger to literally squeegee about half way down the tube towards the pouch. Holding the tube with one hand keeps you from pulling against it and hurting yourself, while the thumb and first finger get the majority of the fluid and fatty tissue to move on down the line and into the pouch like it's supposed to.

Once the majority of the fluid is in the pouch, (majority meaning you won't be able to get all of the fluid or tissue out of the tubes and that's perfectly alright…) you'll unstop the little stopper on top and squeeze the fluid into a measuring cup. The measurements on the side will let you see just how much fluid you had and writing the amount on the chart with the date and time you emptied actually becomes a treat! You will visually see the progress you're making. Every few days the amount measured will be less and less, and you'll feel better every time you see that number getting smaller. Want to know why? Because when your 'numbers' get down to about 10cc or less for the entire day your reconstructive surgeons office will remove the drain tubes. Can we say hallelujah!

Studly became the master drain tube stripper in our household. Twice a day, we'd make the trip up to our bathroom, I'd place the measuring cup and drain chart beside the sink, he'd help me slip out of my pj top, I'd hold the drain tube steady and he'd go to stripping! Now granted, we had to learn our lesson with the drain tubes like everything else. Both of us wound up accidentally pulling the tube the first time. I hollered and jumped, which caused me to holler again, and a few deep breaths later we finally joined forces to attack with stealth. Once we got past that one rough session, we were in business! And by the time Mama felt up to the task a few days later watching us work as a team, I was just about ready to strip the drain tubes on my own. It wasn't easy, but again – it's all about gaining your independence back. Nobody knows my stubborn streak better than my Mama!

Arms down at my sides, Studly slips the pj top back into place and helps with the bottons, and down to the living room and my oh-so-sweet recliner. Another lesson I had to learn – when you begin to sit down, be smart, and hold the tubes away from your butt cheeks. Otherwise, the cheek with slip right through the drain tube line and snag it on the way down. Trrrust me. You don't want to sit your full weight down on a drain tube line. Talk about pulling at stitches and not being able to jump up right quick to correct the problem!

When it comes time to remove the tubes, don't fret. I panicked enough to pop a pain pill on the way to see *Super Doc*, thinking that if the tubes hurt me this bad they would surely hurt coming out. Turns out that all his PA had to do was snip the few stitches holding the tube and my skin together and she pulled it right out. I literally had no feeling when the tube came out and didn't even know she had removed it until she said, "Here, hold onto this for me" and placed the tube and pouch in my lap before walking around the exam table to my other side!

Now I thought my *Studly* would need a pain pill from the look on his face – apparently the part of the tube that was inside of me was approximately eight to twelve inches long and just seeing those inches being pulled out of me was enough to turn his stomach. However, I literally had absolutely no feeling when she removed all four tubes, and once they were out of me, I could immediately move my arms around better and wiggle my back easier almost like I was stretching! The holes in your skin where the tubes are close up immediately and I only leaked a drop or two from each hole while we were still in the exam room.

The ride home was the most comfy ride I'd had yet and as soon as I slipped back into my pj's and settled into the recliner I knew we had crossed one more major milestone. I could sit back without the tubes poking and hurting me, and would rest easier.

That night I tried lying in bed for the very first time. *Studly* and I propped up a mound of pillows because I knew I still couldn't lay flat on my back because of the moved muscles, stitches, weight of my upper torso pushing on those stitches and in general simple soreness. I got to prop next to my *Studly* for the first time in weeks, and I was able to lay there listening to his sweet snores – it was heaven! Now, I didn't make it all night long propped up in bed mind you – it took several hours, and

I did in fact have to go back to the recliner to sleep for the remainder of the night. At least I got a few hours of being able to be in the bed and that was worth it to me.

Each night over the next week, I was able to last longer and longer in bed at night so that eventually I slept from the time I laid my head down to the time the alarm went off each morning. I still had the aches and pains during the night that would wake me up, but at least I had the choice of staying in bed or heading to the recliner if you know what I mean.

# Potty Training ~ *Being Passed in the Fast Lane*

One thing no one warned me about was the fact I would lose total modesty during all of this and I do mean total. I'm about to get real up close and personal with y'all, so pardon me for being blunt, but this is something that needs to be talked about.

The first three weeks after my first round of surgery, I literally could not reach my arms in front or behind me to wipe after going to the bathroom. I had to totally depend on my *Studly* or whichever family member stayed with me and it was like potty training all over again. I couldn't even push my pajama bottoms down either. When I needed to go to the bathroom, it was like a convoy – I announced (really I gave fair warning if it was going to be a #1 or a #2 kinda visit…) that I had to go. Whoever was in charge of me got up, and we went to do my business. Thankfully by the end of the third week, I was able to ease down my pajama bottoms and wipe my front side; however, I wasn't able to wipe my own behind until the fifth week and even then I had to do it from the front side reaching as far back as I could with a wet wipe. See, I told y'all this was like potty training! (Because of the incisions on my back, the moved muscles, and the stitches, it was honestly into the eighth week before I was ever able to wipe from the back. No kidding. Those muscles didn't like to be moved apparently, and they decided to get even with me.)

After the drain tubes were out, I felt like getting out in public again. No more safety pins holding yucky fluid tubes or grenade pouches hooked to the inside of my shirts were an absolute blessing! We put our thinking caps on and tried to figure out where I could go and walk to get a little bit of exercise but also be able to sit down and rest in case I got tired – some place with air conditioning would be nice too, since it was summer time in the South. AH-HA! The mall!

That next morning, I was so excited to get out and move around for the first time in weeks that I was up and dressed in my zip up t-shirt and comfy shorts before seven am. Mama came to pick up my pillow and me (because you'll wind up keeping a pillow behind your back for many, many moons my friends...) and we headed to town. I actually made my first lap with slow steps and not being too out of breath when it happened....another walker passed me. And not just any walker, an elderly woman that looked older than my grandmother zoomed by me so fast she should've gotten a speeding ticket in the fast lane!

My jaw dropped, my eyes about bugged out of my head in absolute shock, I looked over at my Mama and she was grinning from ear to ear at my expression. I asked her in total bewilderment, "Did you see that?!"

She calmly said to me, "Yup – now whatcha gonna do about it?"

Leave it to Mama to bring you back to reality when you need it while still being a cheerleader from the sidelines. By the time I made another half lap around the upper section of the mall, that same elderly woman made her second lap passing me. This time she stopped to ask me what had happened, as it's pretty obvious with me being leaned over a bit and holding my arms up under what used to be my breasts, that something was wrong. In the South, we talk and it's not uncommon for two complete strangers to just strike up a conversation like they've been friends forever. That's exactly what this woman did, she put a hand gingerly on my back and I simply told her I'd just got out in public for the first time since having a double mastectomy due to breast cancer. That's as simple as can be put so I don't drag her through a month and a half worth of diagnosis and surgeries. Her eyes popped out of her head in astonishment and I got a 'bless your heart' and several sweet comments before she took off again like a bat out of hell down the mall.

By the time I finished my second lap around I was working on, she had told the whole food court full of elderly walkers who the 'rookie' was and I had a standing ovation as we passed by. I now had a food court full of cheerleaders in my corner, and every morning we walked, I'd get low fives, uplifting comments, and friendly challenges to see if I could keep up with at least the handicapped scooters. They were slower than some of the walkers, believe me! Much to my Mama and Studly's chagrin, I also got offered a few winks from the elderly men…but they both assured me it was simply because I was the only one in the mall they had a chance of catching. Nothing like being ganged up on, is there?

# Medicinal Margarita's
## *Learning Breast Friends Don't Judge*

It's at times like this when only Mama understands what you really need and that is a jumbo medicinal margarita! We have our local Mexican restaurant hangout in town where everybody knows our name and we never have to ask for our drinks. They see us walk in the door, they pour. We're not sure just who is training whom anymore, but we try not to over think it. In we go, plop down in our assigned seats, and begin to solve the world's problems. It's what we do when medicinal margaritas are flowing, well that and we gossip about our family. Hey, we can talk about our family 'til the sun don't shine. Let anyone else start running their mouths and it's a whole 'nother situation. What I began to realize is this is part of the healing process, too; not exercise, not running back and forth between doctor appointments, not worrying about whether or not the boobs are at the angle they're supposed to be at, but simply sitting down and un-laxing! This is the good stuff, no matter what shape you're in. Enjoy it, let your hair down for a few hours, and call *Studly* and Step-Daddy G to come getcha sorry butts after a few pitchers because after all – you'll have that medicine head feeling after the first pitcher and we don't call them medicinal margaritas for nothing!

One afternoon when I was out and about with a friend, a comment was made about a young woman who passed by us at the grocery store. She had a rack on her that would've drawn ANY body's attention and let me tell y'all something – a month and a half ago; I would have made a similar comment. That day though, it dawned on me: she could've had her breasts cut off due to breast cancer too, and she just might have gone through the same reconstructive surgery I was going through. I knew then I could never look at a woman with obvious implants the same way again. Whether they were showing them off loud and proud, or covering them up in a Nun's habit – I would NEVER judge a woman like that again. She was proud of her breasts, and I actually wished I could be as proud when I finally got mine!

All these thoughts hit me like a ton of bricks and I thought about all the women in my past that I had judged so wrongly and I felt the deepest shame I had ever felt in my life. Here I was, crying to myself at times because I felt so incomplete, so out of control of my life, hurting mentally and physically after such intense surgery, knowing I had even more surgeries to come…and to think I had the gall to judge someone who'd gone through any type of plastic surgery. Right there in the store, I went to boo-hooing and shocked my friend when I spilled my guts about what I'd just realized. Next thing I knew, she was crying right along with me and said she'd never thought about it that way, either. She never had reason to think about seeing a woman with an obvious 'boob job' instead of understanding it just might be due to breast cancer or any other type of debilitating illness which required reconstruction. I think the impact of that moment did us both one helluva favor.

For my twenty-ninth birthday, the family & friends participated in a local breast cancer charity motorcycle ride! It had been a tradition in the making, but now that we had someone directly affected in the pack, it was all the more special. Everyone had pink bras draped on side mirrors or strapped to helmets and windshields and we were rolling down the highways with about five hundred other supporters. Bikers can sometimes look all scruffy, rode-hard-and-put-up-wet, whichever cliché you choose – but know this about us; no other group that stretches from one side of the US to the other loves to participate in charity events as much as we do. We're nothing but big bad teddy bears, in search of a cause! Once we find one, the word spreads like wild fire and here comes the calvery decked out in leathers.

I was nowhere near being able to get on a motorcycle, so a girlfriend in the group volunteered to drive Miss Daisy. She even had pink bras fastened on the back of the headrests, and the convertible top down! When we showed up at this major event in our hometown, everyone realized there was a new survivor amongst the crowd and we got cheers and warm wishes all around. The Blessing of the Bikers commenced with survivors up on stage and heads bowed throughout the whole crowd. Here were all these tough bikers with crocodile tears streaming down weathered cheeks and into wind-blown beards. You would've thought they were looking at us survivors on stage like we were their hero's. My heart overflowed, and I had to ease off stage to go stand next to Studly. He gently put his arm around me, gave me a kiss, and then we all got situated in line for the main ride. No one made a fuss over me, and that's the way I wanted it. In my mind, the survivors or hero's were the ones who'd gave it their all and lost the battle, the ones that had to undergo chemotherapy and radiation, not me.

Off we went through town in a convertible, surrounded by burly bikers sporting pink bras, and we had a blast! I was able to take lots of fun pictures to share with the others. Hey! What-cha-know, if you only take a picture from the neck up, you would never know my boobs were gone!

The second breast cancer charity motorcycle ride turned out not to be a charity at all, but a benefit ride for someone else near and dear to our hearts. The sister-in-law of one of our pack was losing her battle with breast cancer, and the benefit ride in her honor was to raise money and was her last hurrah. She was home from the hospital, sporting a sassy lil' baseball hat, a pink ribbon t-shirt, and gently lifted onto the back of a Trike. I sat on the sidelines this time, in my folding camp chair armed with a pillow. In about an hour and a half, the whole parade was back and we all went into a bar to celebrate. It's times like this that make you truly grateful and remind you how lucky you really are to still be kicking. God Bless the Pink Angels.

# Expansion Here We Come….Fill Em' Up & Feel Like A Woman!

The first week after my drain tubes were removed, I got my first fill up. Now, *Super Doc* had generally explained the process and even joked with us that if I couldn't make it up to his office and wanted to sit in the car that he'd come down to the parking lot to do the chore. Whatever I was comfortable with was fine with him. Hence, the reference to 'fill ups' and 'drive-thrus' so that you're up on my lingo.

Fortunately and unfortunately, I would never have any sensation in my breast mounds so I knew it wouldn't hurt necessarily. Why don't I have sensation? Remember, *Super Doc* scraped out all the insides of my boobs with a pumpkin scoop! That meant nerve endings too, and he wasn't lying. I can literally take my fingernails, scratch hard across my boobs, and not feel the first sensation. Pins-n-needles asleep tingles would at least be something. I feel absolutely nothing. The only thing the surrounding tissue and muscles can feel is pressure if you were to press down. It's pretty wild, but hey – at least my pain was never in my breasts from the front incisions – all the pain was in my sides, and back.

So *Studly* helped me out of my zip up top (easy access for the doc's) and up onto the exam table. Don't you just love that crinkle and crunch of white butcher paper on a roll covering those oh-so-comfy pleather tables? He sat down in his assigned seat, and in came *Super Doc*. With a three inch needle. Aimed at my boobs. A syringe big enough to scare a horse. I raised my eyebrows at *Super Doc* and his Lovely Assistant as if they had better pack a lunch if they thought they were coming at my post surgical body with those things! The funny part was that he had to put an X marks the spot with a magnet over the port where he would stick the needle. The port of the expander implant had a metal ring around the outer lip area and the magnet would latch onto that through my skin and muscle. Only then could he press that magnet down on my skin making an X so that he knew exactly where to aim that three-inch needle.

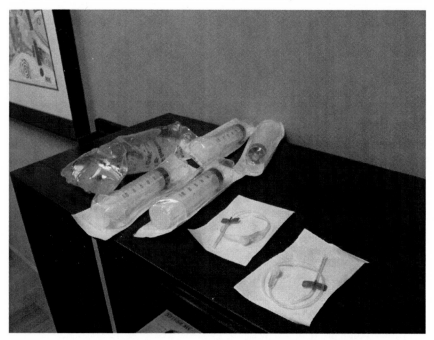

*My Room* at *Super Doc*'s office. 1000mL bag of saline,
four 60cc syringes, two - three inch butterfly needles. All
for the sole purposes of inflating my jugs, and watching
my *Studly* turn green while sliding down the wall!

Now, up til this point my *Studly* was doing just fine. The only look on his face was one that clearly said he was glad it was me and not him on the table that very second! Next thing I knew, *Super Doc* was sticking that three-inch long needle into the X and through the port, only I felt nothing. I mean nothing. There was no pressure, no sting of the needle piercing skin, absolutely nothing. I was dumbfounded and amazed…. *Studly* was green as a gourd and about to pass out.

This is a freaky sight; I'm not about to sugar coat it for you. It's like something out of a horror movie, but without the feeling. That's the only way I can explain it to you. Then I started laughing at the whole situation because my breast mound started blowing up like a hot air balloon – it literally began inflating right before our very eyes! That first fill up, I got over 100 cc of saline injected into each expander implant and walked out of that office like I was the Queen of Sheba. I was on cloud nine and was still in udder amazement that I had something forming under my shirt…get it, udder?!

*Super Doc* helps me off the throne in my room and we go into the Paparazzi room next door to take a few snap shots of the progress. Hmmm…why in the world is my left boob bigger than my right? I don't mean fuller or prettier, I mean the damn thing is almost twice the size of my right! *Super Doc* just grins and says to remember that the goal of the expansion process is not the pretty or cosmetic part; this part is all about stretching out those disconnected & reconnected muscles and breast tissue. Oh yeah, that's right, sorry I forgot *Super Doc*. Therefore, I go ahead and except the fact that over the next several many weeks of expanding my new muscles and skin, I'm going to be completely kaddywhompus.

Don't rock the boat, I'll fall off the left side and sink with this extra water weight!

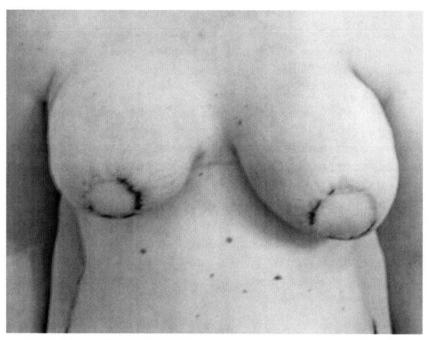

First fill-up of 150cc's Scabs beginning to wash off
around skin flaps, and drain tubes removed!

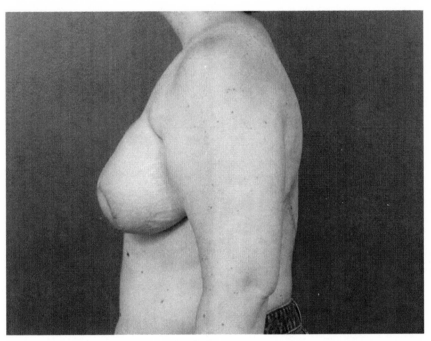

*Super Doc*'s Paparazzi room
Position 3 / 90 degree angle showing left side

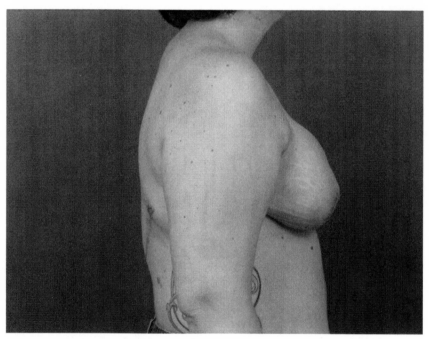

*Super Doc*'s Paparazzi room
Position 6 / 90 degree angle showing right side

As soon as we got in the car, I was ready to shout it to the world about our experience that morning, so I called my Daddy, my Mama, and my Nana. You just can't even begin to imagine it properly; you've just got to witness it for yourself. By the time I finished explaining the events to them they were all rolling laughing! The next day, I showed all three of them the progress that had been made. After all, at this point they'd all seen me before the first injection looking like a flat chested twelve-year-old boy – why not show 'em what progress looks like!

# A Girls Gotta Sparkle ~ *It's all about the accessories, the hair, and pheromones*

Another cool thing about going through expanders is that they're hard enough that you don't jiggle. Truth be told, mine felt like a solid brick across my chest with two mounds. And because of the muscle relocation and incisions none of my former bras was an option. It was unthinkable to have anything pressed against the scars on my back, so I went without a bra…in public no less…and no one was the wiser. How cool is that? Sort of liberating when you've been very dependent on bras since the third grade!

Right after my first fill up, I realized that if I was going out into the world again I might as well try to look pretty. And trust me, no amount of support from family or friends, no amount of clichés, and no amount of previous self assurance helps. What once physically defined you as a woman has been cut off.

In my mind, that would be the equivalent of a man's penis being removed and a doctor taking him through the steps of reconstruction and the stress of trying to get it 'right' again by expanding the remaining skin inch at a time. It's intense, but I knew I wasn't the type of person to stay hidden in doors from the world so I was going to have to do something.

Remember, at this point I'm still having to have help with my showers so it's not like I can lift my arms yet to fix my hair. I started thinking accessories. Hey, a girls gotta sparkle – that's my motto! So on a morning walk around the mall, Mama and I stopped by a little boutique selling head bands. I'm not one to cheat on my hair – I like the whole process of killer hair and time spent in front of the mirror to make it happen. Even a ponytail can rock! Nevertheless, that was out of the question right now and at least headbands are back in style so what the heck. I tried on a few with Mama's help, and picked out several styles that would work with my current hairdo and No Rinse shampoo wet look. It was cute enough and somewhat sexy sleek if you know what I mean.

Next came my earrings and lipstick – those are the two things I simply can't live without on a daily basis, and I still consider myself a bit of a tomboy. I have always loved my earrings and have everything in my jewelry box from studs to chandelier styles; lipstick in every shade possible to suit my skin color. Well look out world, at least my head is back in business if no other part of my body is!

Once I actually felt a little bit pretty, it hit me – with or without boobs, I still have pheromones and hormones and it's been weeks since I was able to get my hands on my Studly! Whoa girl, slow it down....just because you're young and have raging hormones doesn't mean you're physically able to get your groove on just yet....trrrrrust me. So now, it's a completely new torture. Feeling better, looking good, and dang it – staying covered up. Hey, it's part of this whole process. Might as well call a spade a spade and say that it takes a little longer for sex to happen. Sorry girls.

# A Hitch In My Stride ~ *A whole new set*

On a lighter note though, it was somewhat cool to look back at the before and after pictures. There are only three so far – the before, after, and after the first fill up picture. However, looking at the progress that was being made and seeing it sort of like third hand in a photograph instead of just looking down at yourself is interesting to say the least. For the next three weeks and fill ups, we kept digital pictures at home we took ourselves, and *Super Doc* had his set of pictures as well.

We took them just like *Lovely Assistant* took them for us – at different degrees showing the views from the front, right and left sides forty-five and ninety degree angles, and the back. I loved the idea of the pictures because up until this point, all we had were drawn pictures in pamphlets and again we'd felt very much unprepared for what I would look like despite all the talks and research. Now, I had my own set of before and after surgery, and during reconstruction phases. If anyone ever came to me in the future and asked for my help with their breast cancer or mastectomy questions I would be able to help them feel prepared for what they were about to experience. It was during the picture taking around the third fill up that I got the idea to document all of this into more than just a personal scrapbook, and into a book to share with others.

At the third fill up, something happened I was totally unprepared for. I started hurting less than two hours afterwards. I was feeling something when I wasn't supposed to have any sensitivity. My left breast mound felt like stabbing pains were coming from it and my right breast mound was literally pushing into the muscle connecting my pectoral muscle into the under arm muscle which was then in turn hitting a nerve making sparks shoot down to my elbow. It was bad enough to pop a pain pill that night, but I got through it and in the morning, I decided to call *Super Doc*'s office. He assured me it was totally normal for me to 'feel' these side effects and explained them to me in detail.

Turns out the left breast expander was expanded to the point of REALLY stretching the muscles and skin like it was supposed to, and the muscles were having contractions. Huh? My boob is having contractions? He died laughing, and said technically yes – the muscles were contracting due to the constant stretching and that was a good thing because the expanders were doing their job. I told him in return, "Fine. Next time I have a contraction at three a.m. I'm calling you to help me through the Lamaze breathing."

If my boobs are going into contractions, then I do NOT want to see the alien they're about to deliver.

As for the right breast pushing the muscles into the nerve, which was shooting pain to my elbow, that was the expander doing its job again and I simply needed to move that arm around and flex the arm back and forth to un-kink that nerve. So all day, I gently flexed my arm all the way out and half way back in loosening the muscles back up. Sure enough, it worked like a charm and I didn't take any more pain medications!

The fourth week after my surgery I went in for my regular weekly fill up, but *Super Doc* had a perplexed look on his face. He didn't like how my expanders were expanding my skin and muscles. Apparently, they weren't cooperating according to his rules. My expanders were overly expanding on the top portion of my breast mounds and were flat as a board on the underside. *Super Doc* didn't like this one little bit, and I obviously didn't either but with my limited knowledge of how I was supposed to look not helping matters, I didn't realize it wasn't supposed to look like this. I knew that they weren't going to look 'normal' during the expansion phase – the expanders are designed to stretch my skin and muscles out. That's all. They're not designed to be normal shaped permanent implants, and I got over that fact as soon as I saw myself after the mastectomy and first fill up. But I still didn't realize something wasn't quite right.

*Super Doc* had smoke pouring out of his ears as he sat there looking at me bare chested on the exam table for a long time before finally speaking. He decided that what we needed to do was an unexpected surgery. Nothing too wrong or major and easily fixable. He needed to remove the current expanders and install what in laymen's terms is like a double-chambered expander. Something he could inject saline into and fill up the bottoms to stretch out the underside like it was supposed to. He'd have to special order them and it would take less than two weeks to get them in his office, so we'd schedule the surgery for then. Not once in his speech did I doubt his word for a second. *Super Doc* said it needed to be done, and so it was going to be done. I trusted this man with my life or else I would've never let him operate on me to begin with.

This surgery was going to set me back by about two month's time though. Well, I'd just have to suck it up and deal with that despite over how excited I'd been with the progress we had made. Fine, we would simply make progress again. Simple as that.

The surgery itself would be fairly simple: *Super Doc* was going to cut back into the exact same sutures connecting my breast mounds to my flapped nipple area, use a similar syringe to remove all the saline from the expanders so they were empty (sort of like an emptying a water balloon) remove the expanders, and insert the double chambered expanders, stitch me up, and inject the saline into the new expanders to fill them back up. Unfortunately, not the exact same amount of saline would be injected – I would have a little less just to make sure everything was in place as it should be. Then we'd inject all over again to catch me back up to the level of saline cc's I was at before this unexpected surgery. It would take several weeks, but in the end my skin and muscles would be 'right' in *Super Doc*'s eyes, and therefore it was worth it.

After the surgery was over and I woke up from Mama Anesthesia's potion, I was surprised at the feel of my new expanders. As soon as my eyes were open, and I was in my post-op recovery room, I snuck a peek under my bandages and saw that the top and bottom of my breast was nicely rounded like normal. I could actually feel the roundness on the underside of the breast mound through the bandages, even though *Super Doc* forbid me to remove them for a whole week. He wanted to do it himself with the help of Lovely Assistant in his office due to the nature of this beast.

I went home like a good girl and went back to taking sponge baths with the help of my *Studly* and Mama. But you know, living in the South has it's good points…the humidity is always so high in the summer times you can sit still under air conditioning and still perspire at times… this caused my water-proof bandage to come unglued at the top and bottom of my breast mounds. Can you believe that? So naturally, I went ahead and removed it about two days before my one-week check up with *Super Doc*. Hehehe, he knows me and was grinning before he walked through my exam room door. I wouldn't have doubted it if he and Lovely Assistant had a side bet going on whether or not the bandage would be there when I came to see them!

We were all very pleased and actually excited about the new expanders and the immediate difference they made. I got my first fill up that same day and had the whole hot air balloon experience all over again, called my family like I was supposed to do on the way home, and settled back into the routine like we hadn't skipped a beat. The only difference was going to be now when I put on shirt over my mutant phasing boobs,

63

they were shaped more naturally. Gotta luv that lil' bonus! In addition, when we got home, I saw Nana had been by and shoved a big new tub of her chicken salad on the shelf in the fridge. God, she is one amazing woman.

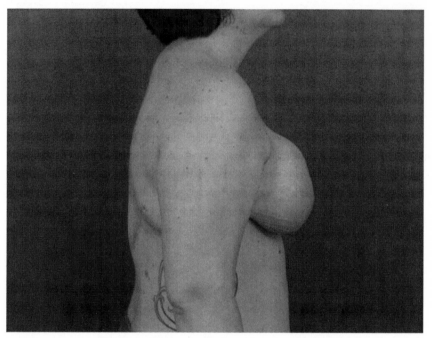

Position 6 / 90 degree angle of right side
Expander implants filling up, and stretching
skin and muscles into lumps

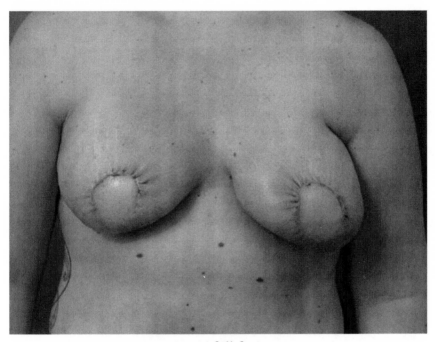

Position 1 / full front pose
Expander implants looking lumpy, but the scabs are
almost washed away! Note the yellow-ish bruise on the
right breast above the skin flap. This happens at times
when the three inch needle is inserted for the fill-ups.

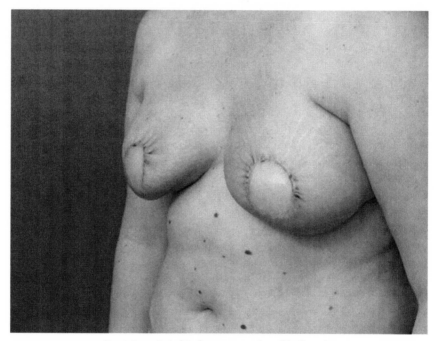

Position 2 / 45 degree angle of left side

# Back To Work ~ *My pillow goes where I go*

On the way home I began thinking about going back to work in a week or two, and realized I couldn't walk in the door not wearing some sort of bra or top under my clothes because the skin was puckered around the skin flap nipple area and it would show through looking very unnatural. A new friend of ours we met at a pool party earlier this summer mentioned her mother went thru a mastectomy and when it was time to wear a bra, she had found an awesome little boutique in the Atlanta area that specialized in cancer patients & mastectomy fittings. I contacted her and *Super Doc*, and both agreed this boutique would be the place to go!

I was pretty excited and made myself a fitting appointment, but then got to thinking about pricing. After all, I would only wear this double-barrel sling shot for a few weeks until I had the next surgery and I would never be able to wear it again. The thing had to be expensive after viewing the boutique's website since it was a specialty undergarment. Then it hit me….my whole goal was to have my same cup size, so why not use my regular bra as a sort of sizing chart! *Super Doc* had been trying to explain to us the whole time that there is no comparison of a normal bra cup vs. injected cc's into the expanders, so I would use my own over-the-shoulder-bolder-holders and show *Super Doc* as we progressed through the fill-up process again! What better way to go, and we'd save some money along the way – WHOO-HOOO! I just love those Ah-Ha kinda moments; don't you?

As soon as we got home, I went upstairs and started stripping...with the help of Studly, hehehe...told y'all he was a big ol' flirt! After he helped me out of the shirt, we tried to put on the bra. Well two things happened; one, the bra wouldn't actually fit around my middle and two, my breast mound was about one and a quarter inches away from touching the inside of the cup. OK, I knew I wasn't going to be the same girth size simply because when *Super Doc* and *Honey Doc* worked on me during the actual double mastectomy they had to remove an attached side of the third latimus dorsi muscle from my back, stretch it back around itself at my sides, and reattach it at my sternum. Nevertheless, it still irked me, believe it or not. Therefore, the muscle overlapping itself made my torso larger in size. I didn't know what size that would actually be (and I could have easily kept my appointment at the boutique just so I could get an accurate fitting and know what size I was) or I could make a field trip to Wally World, and simply buy that little extender for a dollar and thirty seven cents. This part is not rocket science folks.

A few days later, Mama and I went to buy the extender and tested out our lil' theory. Voila! The extender worked like a charm. Yea! Next step was the fashion show; I wanted Mama to help me try on all my work clothes to see what would look natural under the tops. I knew that Mama would be completely honest with me about how I looked in clothes. We had taken a blood oath together years ago that whenever one of us tried on an outfit, we would tell each other the truth and never let the other one wear something frumpy. We took it slow because putting on and taking off clothes is a chore when you're top half is in pain...not to mention how much of a sweat you'll work up even under normal circumstances.

Some clothes looked normal, and some received an "absolutely not" wisecrack from Mama. Those that didn't work for now were folded up and put on a shelf in our closet. These clothes consisted of silk & polyester fitted style shirts. The only ones allowed to hang on the rod were the ones that looked normal over the bra. These were the knitted tops because they were of a thicker material, and wrap style shirts and dresses because I could take a safety pin and close up the top to cover where my old cleavage would normally show.

You see, because my breast mound didn't quite fill up the cup there was a little bulge of bra fabric that looked loose in a way. If you put on a shirt over that loose fabric then it also made the shirt lay an odd way in the chest area. It's the same difference if you spot a woman wearing a bra too small. Y'all know what I'm talking about; I know you've spotted a mound of cleavage spilling out before. This was just the opposite reaction to that effect. So now, I had half the amount of clothes to go to work in, but it was a start and I could mix and match the wardrobe for a month or two until the next surgery. I wasn't about to spend a heap of money on a wardrobe until after the surgery where my expanders came out and my permanent implants were in place. Only then would I know what my true bra and shirt size would be.

We finish the fashion show, and all of a sudden, it dawned on me that the hair on the back of my neck was standing up as if someone or something was glaring at me. I slowly turned around and peeked in the closet, and BAM! I'm eyeball to eyeball with my favorite pair of Levi's. I realized that if I could finally ease clothes on and off my body almost on my own, that I bet I could slip into my favorite old ripped up jeans. I looked at Mama; she looked at me, and sighed in defeat.

For years, my family has begged me to throw out these jeans – y'all, they're torn up like you wouldn't believe, faded from stonewash to almost white, and soft as cotton balls. I've had these jeans since I was in high school and in my mind, they're just now gettinn' broke in good! They were up on a shelf just a little too high for me to reach up and pull down, so I had to beg (and I do mean beg) my Mama to please get my jeans, oh please, oh please, oh please. She rolled her eyes, got them off the shelf, and even though it took me a few seconds longer than normal to slide my legs in so my feet and toes didn't get caught or poke out through the holes, it was so worth it!

I want y'all to know it's all about lil' milestones like this. Sometimes, we are caught up in day to day things like pain, medications, doctor's visits, and the whole nine yards…but every once in a while, something small happens and just knocks your socks off. Not that I would mess up my favorite ensemble by wearing socks or shoes, but you know what I mean.

Hi-ho-hi-ho, it's off to work I go! I was more nervous than a long tailed cat in a room full of rocking chairs, but at least I looked normal walking in the door…except I had a pillow under my arm and a clutch purse in my hand. Of course, I knew I'd be teased about bringing my blankey with me to work, but that's ok. It had been fourteen weeks since the first surgery and my back still couldn't stand hard surfaces because of the eight inch long scars and too sensitive muscles. Even in padded office chairs, the car, and on the couch at home I still had to lean back on a pillow. I personally think it had more to do with than just the incisions; when *Super Doc* sewed my back up after the first surgery my skin puckered and created pockets on either side of the stitches making it look like a biscuit roll (that's what we call it in the South when a woman wears tight shirts and shows fat rolls on her back.) So now I had these fatty lumps on either side of both incisions, and it created pressure on those scars.

*Super Doc* assured me when we did the third surgery removing the expanders and inserting the permanent implants, he would also do liposuction to remove the fatty scar tissue surrounding the incisions so it would look and feel more natural. Oh well, when the muscles were ready then I would know. Until then, appease them with a pillow. As for the clutch pocketbook, I couldn't stand to have something hanging on my shoulder and tucked under my arm at my side. Between the other sore muscles at my sides and having something pushed against the side of my breast it just wasn't happening. Period. So clutch it was, and that's fine with me because I have a slight pocketbook fetish anyways and would get to buy a few more to add to the collection….hey, it's for medicinal purposes ya know! Since I wasn't spending money on bras or clothes, I could rationalize the clutches.

Now y'all, we are all human and I knew I would get strange reactions from coworkers on my first day back to work. Especially from people I hadn't seen during the past three months. And every one of the people had the exact same reaction to me – their eyes went to my chest first, and my face last. My chest was like a magnet, and apparently, it surprised a few people that I wasn't bandaged up like a mummy walking with an IV tower. They can't help it, and I knew it, but it still made me blush and got on my nerves. Oh well, just take a breath and remind yourself that if the shoe was on the other foot I might be doing the same thing.

One thing that helped was immediately saying hello and either sticking my hand out for a handshake, or lightly reaching out for a side hug. That sort of got their attention back to my face. Also, I didn't walk around our floor or any of the other floors in the building – I went straight to my dept and began working. It saved time because otherwise I would've been bombarded with people asking the same questions and repeating the same story until I was blue in the face.

The next day was my normal Tuesday fill-up. *Studly* and I spoke with *Super Doc* and *Lovely Assistant*, explaining my theory of wearing my normal bra as a guide to just how many more injections it would take to fill up my normal cup. They loved the idea, and took a mental note of what I looked like before the fill-up and after. Yup, this was a great plan in their mind and we'd keep it up until I fit in the cup again. *Super Doc* even gave us his guesstimate; two more injections and we'd stop and give my skin time to expand and prep for the next surgery. Now, I had 750cc in each expander implant. *Super Doc* explained that in the USA, the largest legal implant they could order is an 800cc implant.

That was fine with us, because the fill up he'd just given me put me about half an inch from the inside of my bra cup and another 50cc's and I'd be at my normal size. *Super Doc* also explained to us that at next Tuesday's fill-up, he would *over-expand* me by giving me another 100cc's. This would put me at 850cc's, and the reason for the over expansion is because he needs more room and skin to work with when he removed the expanders and inserted the permanent implants. The extra skin would be removed just like from the second surgery. He

71

would go crazy with the blue tattoos again and cut the extra skin from around the nipple skin flap.

Now, my left breast was still slightly bigger than my right; however, he'd take care of that during the next surgery. All was good in *Super Doc*'s eyes, so *Studly* and I went back to work. Later that Tuesday night, the discomfort from the injection and my muscles and skin being stretched got to be just about unbearable. I was hurting enough that I took a pain pill if that tells you anything, because I had not taken a pain pill in the past six weeks from the second surgery. Even then, the post-op nurse had made me eat crackers so I could take one pain pill there at the hospital after surgery before she would release me for the ride home. No, she didn't have any of Nana's chicken salad to go on top of it, either.

Other than that, I hadn't felt bad enough to take a pain pill. But this was just about too much, and sure enough the next morning I couldn't go into work. It took me about 36 hours to feel ok again. The muscles and skin had stretched and finally given in so to speak and I didn't take any more pain pills after that. I went back into work Thursday and Friday like normal.

Since I was feeling better, *Studly* and I went for a test drive. He was going to have to begin traveling with his work on and off for the next six weeks, and I was either going to have to drive myself or have a family member drive me back and forth into the big city. I wasn't about to ask anyone in the family to do that simply because it's twenty-eight miles one way from our driveway into where we both work. Not to mention the economy isn't the greatest we've ever seen and gas prices were continuing to climb.

We drove around the neighborhood and onto the major highway in our town, and even though it wasn't the most comfortable feeling in the world to my stiff torso, I realized that I could actually do it. *Studly* assured me even though he knew I was nervous not only for myself but also for other drivers, I wasn't a danger on the road. He's the most logical person I know, and I knew he wouldn't BS me. If he says ok, then it's ok.

# Overexpansion ~ *The Last Fill Up*

The next Tuesday came and I drove him to the airport before going in for my over expansion and last injection before the third surgery. Now, I was still a bit sore from the last injection simply because up until then I hadn't been that large before. I definitely felt like I'd been over expanded. Not only was I walking around *Super Doc*'s office like I had two watermelons attached to my chest, I felt like too!

I went out to the car and just sat there in the parking lot while I made the mandatory phone calls; *Studly* got a voice message on his cell phone he could listen to once his plane landed, then Daddy, Mama, and Nana were next. It took me about ten minutes sitting there making phone calls before I could crank the car and head onto the roads. As soon as I turned the wheel pulling out of the parking space, I knew – this wasn't going to be a peaceful drive. I couldn't hold my arms normally, they had to over compensate for the big balloon sized boobs. I couldn't make turns easily because it hurt to twist my arms over each other while holding onto the steering wheel. My back felt like it was on fire because the muscles were being pulled even further than they were the week before, and I knew I had to make it home as quickly and safely as I could. There would be no going back to work this day.

As soon as I hit a red light, I made a quick call into work to talk with my boss. I explained (much to his cringing) what the doctor had done and that I was going straight home and wouldn't be able to make it into work.

As soon as I got home and into comfy pj's, I called everyone back and let them know I was at home. Yes I'll be ok, no I don't think I need anyone to babysit me, yes I promise to call if I get any worse, blahblahblah. Wednesday came and went, and I was still not better. I knew from before it would take about thirty-six hours for the skin and muscle to stretch so maybe later on that day I would feel a bit better. Nope. Thursday came and went, still no change. Each day I was taking my pain pills, trying as best as I could to do a few light stretches with my arms and back to get those stiff muscles warmed up, and still sleeping upright in the recliner because that position felt the best to my aching body.

I was even waking up anytime between one am and three am, to take a pain pill as directed so that I stayed ahead of the pain. Not that I needed an alarm clock because honestly I wasn't sleeping all that much anyways. I could last for about two hours at the most before I woke up in the recliner and had to move around simply because I was so stiff and sore.

Friday morning at five a.m., I woke up in absolute agony. Because I hadn't slept for more than a few hours the past few nights, my body had literally just given out and I had slept all night long. Unfortunately, that meant I had missed my pain pill during the night and hadn't moved around during the night either. I sat there not able to move; I couldn't take a normal breath because every time I breathed in it felt like a knife was stabbing into my back, the muscles and skin were stretching to the point I thought I'd split wide open, and the tears wouldn't stop flowing.

To make matters worse, I had gotten careless and didn't place the cordless phone beside me where I could call for help if I needed it. Right now, I needed help and I was hurting worse than I had when I woke up from the double mastectomy. All I could do was keep repeating in my mind, do not panic - do not panic - do not panic. It took me fifteen minutes, but I was able to slowly wiggle my way out of the recliner to the phone laying on the coffee table in our living room. I called my Daddy first, and it was all I could do trying to tell him something was terribly wrong and I had to have some help. He said he would be here as quickly as his car could carry him, and then I called *Super Doc's* office and left him a voice message that was close to hysterics.

I was on the phone with *Studly* when Daddy walked into our front door. Bless his heart, he already felt guilty because he had to leave me to work out of town for the week, now I was in serious pain and he couldn't get to me when I needed him. I assured him I'd made the right phone calls, Daddy was here now, and as soon as *Super Doc* called back, I would call him and let him know what the Doc has said. Don't panic – stay there out of state until we knew exactly what was going on – and if he needed to come home, I promised I would let him know. Yeah, right. *Studly* made the first available flight arrangements that morning to come home.

Daddy knew I needed food in my stomach before I took a pain pill, so we crammed a biscuit down my throat and popped two pain pills for good measure. It took about thirty minutes for the pain pills to kick in, but when they did boy did I feel better. Normally, if I take one pain pill I get very drowsy and can fall asleep standing up if it tells you anything. I wasn't even drowsy. About three hours and another pain pill later, *Super Doc* called back. His office had just opened and he got his voice messages.

By now I was much more calm, and was able to tell him how I'd felt when I woke up and that it had been three pain pills later and we both agreed it was because I had been sore before, over expanded on top of the soreness that was already present, and that I had missed my pain pill during the night. However, if the pain got worse again to call him and I should come into his office so he could take a look. I called *Studly* back and let him know everything was manageable again, and I didn't think there was any reason for him to rush home but he said absolutely not, he had made his flight arrangement and he'd be back in the airport today.

Little did we know that later on around lunchtime we would be dealing with more rain that our county had ever seen. Friday, Saturday, and Sunday we had over twenty inches of rain, major creeks and rivers overflowed their banks, and had some portions of our county flooded to the tips of rooftops. The news stations called it the Flood of 2009, for the metro Atlanta area and we were declared a Disaster Area. Interstates and roads close to water supplies were barricaded because floodwaters created monstrous rapids shutting off all exits around county lines. We all lost power several times, but the main concern was water. Sunday night, water pipes had burst and been contaminated for the whole county.

We didn't have any sort of flood damage at our house, and for that we were very blessed and thankful. All weekend long we surfed the news channels, I laid in the recliner and hurt like the dickens despite pain pills, and we waited for the floodwaters to descend. Grocery and convenient stores sold out of bottled water and bare necessities. No one made it into work because either the interstates were still under water or businesses were closed until water supplies were repaired.

Each morning and afternoon I was on the phone with my boss, giving him an update on how I felt and no I couldn't make it into work either because of pain or because the state D.O.T. hadn't opened up interstates and back roads. Finally, Wednesday late afternoon I felt like I might be moving around and feeling better. At least to where I was down to only taking half a pain pill at a time instead of a whole pill as called for. Thursday morning I was back at work. It had been a week and a half since my last appointment with *Super Doc*, and I was still looking pale and moving very slow and careful. I had found out the slightest odd movement made pain shoot through my back and chest. Bending over was out of the option because I felt top heavy enough that I was scared of falling over. Sneezing and coughing was the worst, each time it happened I felt like I would split my skin open at the scar lines. Not a pretty picture to tell, but that's just how it was. The over expansion was a bitch. No other way to describe it.

Friday through Sunday, *Studly* had taken the kids to the mountains for a weekend getaway and I was grateful for a nice, long, relaxing weekend to help me recover. It had taken a week and a half to get the skin and muscles to relax after the over expansion, and I didn't quite feel up to my normal self just yet. I certainly wouldn't be comfortable anywhere but at home in my own recliner and *Studly* understood that.

Sunday morning I woke up feeling better than I had in weeks! I took one more full pain pill at breakfast, but knew I would go back to only taking half a pill at lunch and dinner, and hopefully be off the pain pills all together in another day or three.

Within a few days, sure enough I was back to feeling myself again; however, certain things happened to remind me I wasn't 100 percent just yet. Number one - I bent over to pick up a load of towels on the floor in the laundry room and just the stretching and the lifting pulled me all out of whack. It felt like I got caught up between two gorilla's and they played tug-of-war with my aching torso. For days I felt the effects that one little bitty load of laundry did to me. Number two – it took that happening to make me realize one wrong move would put me down for days. Sneezing and laundry – lessons learned the hard way.

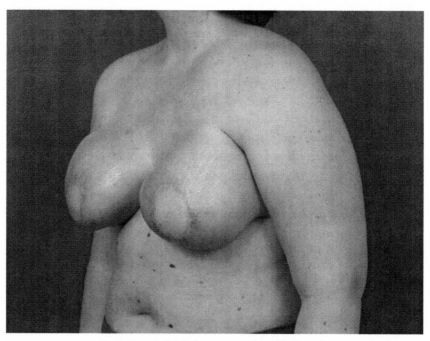

Position 2 / 45 degree angle of left side
Over expanded by 50ccs for the next month, in
order for skin and muscles to fully stretch out

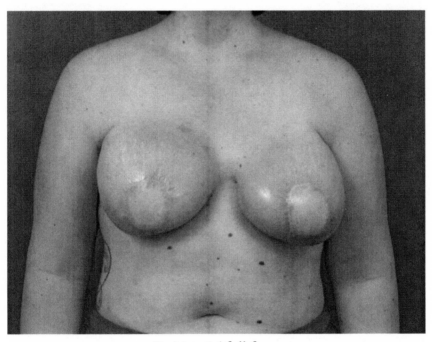

Position 1 / full front
Over expanded by 50cc's Note shiny skin – this is due to the fact
that the skin is stretched so tightly over the expander implants

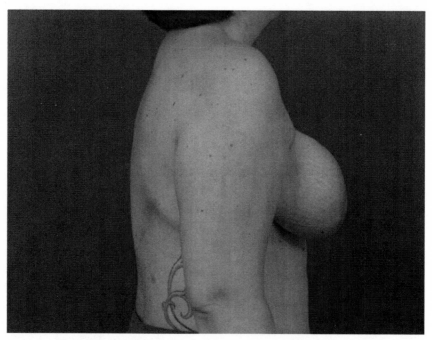

Position 6 / 90 degree angel of right side
You can see a difference now that the second expanders
were installed by the way the underside of the breast is
rounded out normally, and not flat like before.

# Permanent Shock

I went back to *Super Doc* on the fourth week after my over-expansion, and found out I couldn't have my cake and eat it, too. He needed the extra skin to work with for the removal of the expanders and insertion of the implants, and because my skin flaps would also still need to be large enough after this surgery for him to reconstruct the nipples, we were down to one decision or the other: use the 800cc implants or have smaller nipples. It wouldn't be both.

Now y'all, at this point in time I'm just now beginning to feel like I've been put through the ringer and still have several more rounds to look forward to and I'm about tired of all this mess. Simply put, I'm beginning to develop a temper. Alright; so I already have a temper and I'm actually getting a little bitchy. Po-tay-to, pa-ta-to. I'm just tired of constantly having to make sacrifices when I didn't ask for this crap to begin with! But you know what, by the end of the day it didn't matter. Know why? Because I went home and realized after I looked at all the before and so-far-after pictures that 50cc's don't make a hill of beans and I filled out my bra more than I ever had before because the girls were perky and not sagging in a race to my belly button!

Either way, it's not a decision I had to make right that very second…it would be something to think about in a few days at the third surgery. *Super Doc* even let me know that he would have both 800cc and 750cc implants on the surgical table so that if he was able to use the 800cc implants he would – otherwise, it's the 750cc.

I hadn't made it back to work a full week before I realized just what the term disabled really meant. I couldn't lift much more than a laptop computer, or a ream of copy paper. I sure as heck couldn't bend over to un-jam the copy machine or even think about pushing the cart around to deliver files and binders. In addition, if I happened to drop my pen off my desk, I could forget about bending down to pick it up without feeling everything in my upper torso pull and stretch in ways you shouldn't ever have to feel your own muscles.

If I had been rich or a lottery winner, you bet your sweet ass I would've stayed out of work for the duration. I'm dead serious, y'all – I couldn't function as I used to at work before having these surgeries. It simply wasn't time for me to be back at work yet. But, that didn't matter because I'd used up my medical leave of absence time, my team at work needed me, and if I had continued to stay out of work my paycheck would be cut down to only 60 percent. Riiight, as if I could afford that with a growing stack of medical bills on top of our normal household budget. Therefore, it is what it is – I sucked it up and went about my job – even if I did it delicately.

Know what else I found out? It did not hurt me to ask the guys at work for help. I was surrounded by men who wanted to help any way they could and it made them feel good to be able to do something for the pitiful lil' lady.....Hehehe, ok – so I milked it a little while and let them carry my books so to speak. They never knew the difference! All kidding aside...my advice to anybody about to go thru these types of procedures would be to stay home until you were DONE if you were financially able. It's going to make things tougher when you push yourself too soon; however, you're already tough if you're going through this ordeal and we both know you can suck it up and make it! It's a judgment call and one only you can make.

One of my biggest concerns going into my third surgery was what if the permanent implants aren't perfect. What if *Super Doc* installs those puppies and they don't look like I thought they would…hell, they're supposed to be PERMANENT! I don't want to live with some foreign objects in my chest if they don't look how I WANT them to look. *Super Doc* let me know right quick that if once I healed from this upcoming surgery and if I didn't like the outcome then he would remove the implants and do something different. Therefore, I had a 50/50 shot here. I would either like them or I wouldn't…and if I didn't, then it was fixable. I might have to live with them until he could get around to fixing them; but they were fixable. Fair enough, Doc. Let's do this.

By now, we're all pro's in my family when it comes to pre-op visits and the hospitals procedures of pre-surgical tasks. *Studly* and I get to the hospital an hour and a half before my surgery time, the fam-dam-ily waits in the surgery waiting room and entertains the masses – I wake up trying to remember to play nice instead of biting heads off post-anesthesia. Ready, set, hut-hut-hut.

But this time, we were in a completely different hospital with a different surgical team and I got a surprise. The surgical nurse came into my pre-op room when it was time to wheel me back, told me to kiss my *Studly* bye, and as soon as she turned my bed around the corner she slammed on the brakes and told me a secret. She said, "Girlfriend to girlfriend, I see your acne and I know you haven't been able to cure it for quite some time. I had the EXACT same type of acne and found a way to cure mine in only two months!"

Now, at this point in time I haven't mentioned my acne to you because I didn't think it had anything to do with my boobs. I spent over 7 yrs with a flawless complexion, but the past few months after surgery I found out I had developed Nodule acne and it was on my neck and jaw-line. Nothing I did would get rid of it…except super duper antibiotics and those were only prescribed for about 10 days after each surgery to prevent infection from setting in…and different dermatologists tell you different things about this type of acne. It was at times painful, and I was beginning to worry about the acne scarring my skin. Yet, this one surgical nurse had taken one look at me and knew exactly what the problem was and how to cure it.

HALLELUJAH! She said to try a product called Murad, specifically made for adult acne, and she gave me the name of her skin aesthetician. Not a dermatologist – but an aesthetician. Apparently, only two or three months of using this product will not only clear the Nodule acne up, but also keep it from coming back. It sounded exactly like what I'd been looking for, and so she wrote down the info to give to my *Studly* after the surgery. What a gal!

When we busted into the operating room, there was my sacrificial pedestal just waiting for me to strike a pose on. This time as I eased from the bed to the table, I received the royal treatment….Oooh-Weee, I had heated blankets so my tush didn't freeze and fall off on the floor and I wasn't asked to strip out of my sexy hospital gown before being put to sleep! Now that's service, y'all – and other hospitals need to learn from these folks! That nurse had me totally covered with only my nose sticking out of that mound of blankets until finally the anesthesiologist asked me to say night-night.

Now, every doctor I've ever heard on TV says that you don't dream while you're under anesthesia. Those doctor shows let you watch surgeries being performed, with electrodes hooked up to the brain to scan waves, blahblahblah. I'm telling you right now – and if I'm lying, I'm dying – I had a dream while I was put under. It didn't happen until close to the end of my surgery, and I know this for a fact because of the way the dream happened.

I was alone and walking along a sidewalk when all of a sudden I passed in front of a beige colored metal building. There on the opposite side of the street on the other sidewalk was a family of four. They all had dark hair, and were sort of stopped and just staring back at me. I knew they were a family because they touched and leaned on each other like only families do. All of a sudden, all four of them reached a hand apiece out towards me, like they were asking me join them without ever saying a word.

In the dream, I felt so very compelled to go to them. I firmly remember that feeling – it was the strongest feeling I have ever had in a dream, and I have pretty graphic dreams. I reached out to the family and they all smiled the kind of smile that relaxes your whole face with love and understanding. I chose them and just as I was walking towards them, I literally felt a force pulling me backwards. Something pulling me away from the comfort and love I so desperately wanted to be surrounded by.

I woke up to the sound of beeping monitors, a sore throat which I knew immediately was from the trachea tube, and looking at *Super Doc's* surprised face and then his quickly retreating backside.

Uh-huh…something was up and he did not want to be around when I was fully lucid. The nurse leaned over and called my name to get my attention, and the first thing that flew out of my mouth was, "Did he use the 800cc implants?"

She flips thru the chart (like she didn't know – who's she trying to fool?) and tells me as it turns out, he wasn't able to keep the 800cc implants in because when he tried to stitch up my skin flaps once he installed them, they were too big to the point it was tearing the skin from the stitches. That meant that the skin flap wouldn't heal at all – it would turn black and die.

I thought I had prepared myself for this moment – I thought I had psyched myself into a better reaction, but I just lost it right there in recovery. Her eyes got big and bless her heart; she just didn't know what to do! I started bawling like a big baby, pitching a hissy fit because my jugs weren't 50cc's bigger. Was it not enough that part of my womanhood had been cut off? Was it not enough that I'd already been through painful expansions? How about the teeny-tiny fact that I just wanted to look and be me again?

Looking back, it didn't matter that they were so friggin' big that laying flat on my back I couldn't look down and see my toes over the suckers. I admit it; I had a drama-queen moment. It took them wheeling me back into a post-op recovery room and my *Studly* wiping my tears up with his shirt sleeve, that he'd never be able to put his big paws around the massive things anyways, so what in the world was I upset over! I finally laughed, then realized I had to pee like a rushing race horse but was still too doped up to move myself. He got a kick out of hauling my butt out of the chair and onto the toilet. Thank goodness, I still had that sexy hospital gown on because the second I sat down my bladder let loose and all was right with the world again.

# S-T-R-E-T-C-H

The first twenty-four hours after surgery, I didn't have any real pain and only took one pain pill. Even that was because the nurse made me take one before leaving the hospital for the ride home! I was just extremely sore in my shoulders and arms. I felt like I'd been beat with a baseball bat to be perfectly honest.

The second morning after surgery, I woke myself up in the recliner S-T-R-E-T-C-H-I-N-G! I will never forget that one moment: not only was I stretching like Stretch-Armstrong, I scared myself into alertness. I wasn't supposed to be stretching. I hadn't been able to stretch since the first surgery months ago! Huh, I thought – no one was around to tell me not to – so I eased my arms out to my sides again and gingerly stretched and my God, it felt incredible. I must've stretched, moaned, and groaned for what seemed like several minutes...then I heard my Studly's throat clear from the stairs leading down to our living room and the biggest smile on his face I'd seen in forever. He understood, and he'd been watching the whole time from the top of the staircase. I couldn't tell which of us was more excited. If you don't get just how important that stretch was then let me tell you – it's a major milestone to be able to stretch and use muscles when you haven't been able to for many, many moons!

I was feeling so good in fact, that I wanted to make a trip up to our cabin for the weekend. We decided to ask some friends of ours to join us and we all made the hour road trip to the mountains. Yup, Nana's chicken salad came right along with us. While we were up there, my waterproof and super glued on bandage just happened to fall off. Must've been the lil' humidity fairies that did it. But when the bandage came off, my jaw dropped.

I knew I'd see post-surgical gunk and maybe some dried blood, but I was not prepared to see a monster in the mirror. The shock began to fade, and the tears began to fall. I hollered for my *Studly* to join me in the bathroom, and when even his face fell and showed horror and shock, it was just too much. Both breast mounds were lumpy, sagging, nipples weren't centered, and the left breast was literally pointing towards the left. I was devastated.

If you think the boobs and skin flaps were too much reality, you should've seen this. All my fears about having permanent implants had just come true and slapped me in the face. I did the only thing I could – I picked up the cell phone and called the emergency line for *Super Doc*. The on-call nurse whom answered the phone listened to my situation, and assured me this was not the first time she had heard similar remarks. I had a follow-up appointment to see *Super Doc* the next day anyways, and nothing could be done to my breast mounds for weeks until the skin flaps healed enough to be cut on again.

She rearranged my appointment time however to come in as the first patient of the day. To make matters worse, when the bandage came off it pulled the top layer of skin off my eight inch scars from top to bottom because some goofball in the surgery room applied the edges of the bandage to the scars. Someone in the OR obviously had cerebral flatulence during my time on the sacrificial slab. Well, it wasn't a brain surgeon I was working with!

The next morning, I march into *Super Doc*'s office and started stripping off clothes on the way back to the exam room – even *Super Doc* was surprised; however, he also very calmly informed me that he'd seen this happen many times before. Everyone heals differently, and what my breast mounds had just gone through was different than the surgeries before. No matter what I looked like, he wasn't about to put me under anesthesia again so soon. We had to have healthy and healed skin to work with. Right now, it was too soon after surgery to cut on me again. Simple as that and no way around it.

Therefore, he gave me an honest assessment, and told me that the next surgery didn't need to happen for ninety days. Great. Ninety days of seeing myself look like a monster in the mirror would do wonders for my already beaten down self-esteem. I could hardly look at myself in the mirror – I looked that bad – and I wouldn't let my *Studly* see me anymore than he already had.

Now I understood why some women don't want their *Studly's* to see them give birth. Some things might look like a miracle to one person, and to some it's a sight that will scar them for the rest of their lives. This was THAT moment. Top all of that off with the bit of news that it may take two additional surgeries to correct this problem and I was faced with five more surgeries to go, when I thought I only had two more. I literally felt like I was being punished and had to live with making a decision that was wrong and would haunt me for the rest of my life.

To my surprise, over the next three months everything that *Super Doc* told me would happen really did. My skin and muscles finally relaxed around the new implants and accepted that they weren't going anywhere. When that happened, the sagging went away because the skin and muscles conformed to the shape of the implants. The lumps evened out to quite a nice rack if I do say so myself, and I went into see *Super Doc* with a brand new attitude.

Between the third and fourth surgery, I was feeling pretty good and simply aching for a motorcycle ride. Enough was enough. I needed a fix. Studly just happened to get an early Christmas present – a new set of extra loud, supped-up pipes for the Harley! A ride just around town was just what the doctor ordered for the pipes and me. If you've ever been a passenger on a motorcycle, you know there is a proper way to mount and dismount. Try doing it, with your arms being less than useful and thighs a bit flabby from sitting while your body healed up over the past few months. It's pretty comical! Studly kept the bike still while I tried leaning and climbing first on the pegs, then on him trying to get onto the passenger seat. Finally situated, we eased out of the driveway and onto the road to freedom. The first thing I noticed was the wind pressure pushing against my chest. Even with Studly in front of me, the force of the wind was causing me to try and overcompensate by straining my back muscles and lean forward to keep an upright position. Next thing I noticed was that my normal hands relaxed on my thighs or knees wasn't going to happen. Between keeping my distance from slamming into Studly in case he had to put on the brakes, the force of the wind, and a leather jacket confining my torso at the same time it was simply not right yet. We eased up to the first red light, and I knocked the front of my helmet against the back of his and said let's go home. We went around the block and back in the driveway in about three minutes. So much for that, but hey – if you're not ready then you're simply not ready. No one knows their body better then themselves. Mine wasn't up to this just yet.

Speaking of which, it was now time to dismount. Riiight. OK, how to do this without burning a leg on pipes or laying the bike flat on the driveway. I had to think quick because I couldn't use my arms to pull my body weight or push against his shoulders. We tried me standing straight up on both pegs, I tried throwing my right leg up and over, but wound up knocking him silly in the head. *Studly* braced for impact, I stretched my left leg out as far as I could reach on tiptoes and then slid off none too gracefully. A few quick hops on my left leg to keep from busting my butt, and the dismount was complete. Mary-Lou Retton would die laughing if she could see this!

Now y'all may be thinking this is what I get for even temping something this stupid; think all you want to until smoke comes pouring outta your ears! You don't know what you can do until you try it. And if you try it and it hurts, well then you know not to do it again...until you think you're feeling frisky and willing to take another chance. Either way, experimenting is the only way you'll know for sure.

It took me going through weeks of seeing myself as Mr. Hyde, before Dr. Jekyll finally appeared. Once the worst was over with and the girls began to shape up, I started laughing at myself. Even my *Studly* started teasing and laughing with me again. I would stand in front of the vanity getting ready for work without a bra on, and catch him looking at me – then he'd snort and smirk like he was trying to keep a laugh from coming out and I'd have to throw the hairbrush at him. It became a routine and I got my throwing arm back in shape!

*Super Doc* said he agreed it was time for me to begin stretching and waking up muscles I hadn't used in almost a year now. We both thought of exercises I could do, and it dawned on both of us that there still wasn't much I could do because of the back muscles that had been cut, wrapped around themselves at my rib cage, and reattached to my front side! He told me to take any exercise very slowly, even if I felt like it was fine, and give myself a day or two in between whatever I chose to see how it really felt, before moving on again. Sound advice if I've ever heard it! So I began thinking of how I could simply stretch muscles without actually lifting free weights. I still couldn't pick up, push, or pull on hardly anything. Stretching empty handed was going to be it for a while, so I thought I was just out of luck. Ah-Ha! Yoga! For dummies or beginners preferably, and without anything that demanded I become a twisted pretzel, thank you very much.

I didn't have to search very long, because the wife of a co-worker chose that very week to begin teaching free yoga lessons in an empty room of our building. After signing up, I decided to go talk to her early and in private before the first lesson began. Miss Flex was astounded to have a freshly stitched patient among her group, and decided to show me the routine first to see which poses I could do and which ones I could not. Pose by pose we went, and as long as I took it slow and easy I found I could in fact do almost all of them! The ones I couldn't even stand to think about had to do with me laying on my back or bending too far forward.

When the class began, I felt somewhat confident that this was going to be an eye opener one way or the other. Sure enough, forty five minutes later I was stretched out all loosey-goosey and never even broke a sweat. Now that's what I'm talkin' bout girls! Miss Flex even said she would work on customizing a few poses to see if it helped the skin and muscles surrounding my scars, and see me next week. I waited a day or two like Super Doc suggested, and sure enough the muscles protested but didn't complain too much about me finally waking them up. The next week rolled around, and I be-bopped into the yoga room where Miss Flex was waiting for me. She was true to her word, and explained how her Master had also had a double mastectomy and reconstructive surgeries years ago, and had personally found a few modified poses that helped more than others. Here we went a-stretchin', and when others lay on their backs, I kept right on doing my special poses. Worked like a charm, and in a few weeks time I could feel my muscles gaining strength simply from being stretched out! Now I understand why yoga can become so addicting – you can get an incredible workout and never break a sweat. Fab-a-lus for us girls, because if we were to go to a gym for a workout, it would take twice as long because of showers and hair drying.

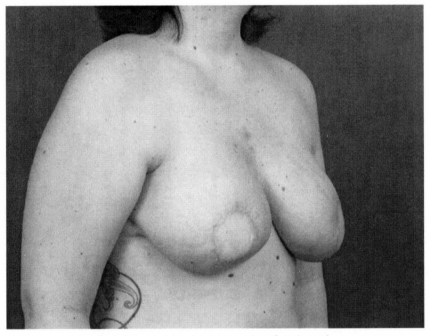

Position 7 / 45 degree angle of right side
Permanent implants not shaped like normal, skin and
muscles hadn't accepted the new implants just yet. See
the red dot in the center of my chest? That's where *Super
Doc* stapled the blind over my chest during surgery!

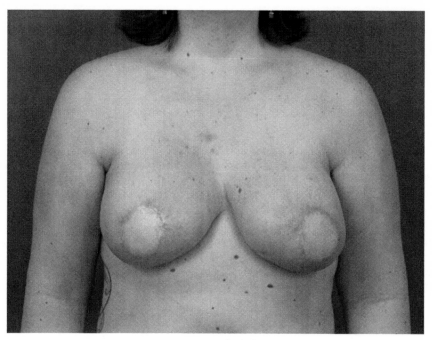

Position 1 / full front
You can see the difference in the position of the left breast
vs. the right. The left breast was pointing outward, instead
of pointing towards the center. Also, the small amount
of excess skin on the left breast allowed it to sag.

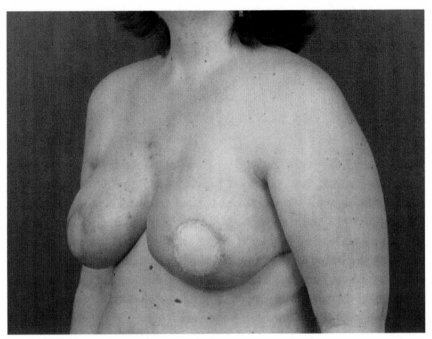

Position 2 / 45 degree angle
Left breast pointing toward the camera saying, Cheese!

# Boob-attude Adjustment *The Vegas Rule Applies ~ What happens in the OR stays in the OR!*

At the ninety day mark, *Super Doc* declared me ready for surgery again and gave me the best news I'd heard in months! After taking my measurements with his super secret tape measure, *Super Doc* said he felt confident he could simply cut the left breast skin flap about three-fourths of the way off and lay it over – remove the excess skin that was allowing my breast to lean too much off center and to the left – then simply stitch me back up. Voila! I had healed and shaped up so naturally in the three months since my last surgery that the simple procedure was all he had to do to make the adjustments!

After I healed up from the adjustment surgery, he said he also felt confident he would have the perfect amount of skin flaps left to make the nipple reconstruction in only one surgery as well. Sweet Jesus – two surgeries vs. five! Folks, it just doesn't get much better than that sometimes. I shook that man's hand and just about jumped all over him in the exam room topless I was so happy! He had stuck by me through it all, lived up to every promise, and kept my crazy ass grounded on a level playing field since the beginning.

This time, as excited as I was about the news he'd just laid on me, I kept myself in-check enough to say that even if he couldn't wrap up my reconstruction in two surgeries that it just didn't matter to me anymore. I knew I was in good hands; I had complete faith in him, and that if we had another complication that resulted in another setback that it would be ok, too. I was in it with him for the long run and we didn't need to set timelines for each other anymore. When he was satisfied with his work, and when he let me know I was complete – only then would we really be done. Not one second sooner. I wish y'all could've seen his face when I said that. His face lit up like the fourth of July! I was proud that I could make his day, and I was proud he was MY *Super Doc*.

I have to admit ahead of time, this next surgery was my favorite. In addition, it wasn't even the final step in the long process. *Super Doc* let me know that since I didn't have feeling in my breasts anyways, that I could stay awake for the adjustment of the left breast tissue. Seriously! I know some people are scared of needles or would never want to see what's happening in an OR room; I'm simply not one of them. I love watching surgeries because I think they're absolutely fascinating and begged *Super Doc* to finally video tape this one since it wasn't going to be anything major.

Not only would he not do that, he wouldn't even let me watch or put a mirror overhead so I could look down upon myself during the surgery. Brat. Why does he gets to see all the good stuff and I don't? Turns out, I even had some of the same nurses and Anesthesiologists as before so it was almost like being around friends welcoming me back and catching up on all the good gossip.

When I was rolled into the OR and climbed onto my pedestal, I was thrilled to be able to help the team by moving this way and that, placing my arms just so-so on the table and strapping in. It was pretty cool just laying there jibber jabbering away with the surgical team and checking out the OR while waiting on *Super Doc* to come on down.

When he walked into the room, the fun began…even though they were letting me stay awake, I still received a lil' dose of happy juice to keep me sedated and calm – after all, my hyper self didn't need to be able to twitch and move around on the table when *Super Doc* had a sharp object in his hand! In no time at all, I was bantering away at him for not allowing me to see what was happening and telling him there was no reason he couldn't remove the blind from my chest. I even promised to be a 'good girl' and quit talking and making him laugh – but oh, noooo.

Fine, I kept right on keeping the surgical team entertained and snickering at me. Now, the doors to the OR were on my right hand side and beside the doors was the biggest digital clock I'd ever seen. Looking around the OR I saw mirrors in the other three corners pointed towards that clock so that at any angle the surgical team simply had to look at the corners to tell the time. The whole time I'm being operated on, I was teasing *Super Doc* that he was five minutes behind. He kept telling me that next time he operated on me he was going to knock my butt out!

There was about a ten minute time period that I dozed off into lalaland from the sedative and that's when the fun began. Apparently, a lil' bit of truth serum was in the drug I had in my IV because I started telling *Super Doc* and the whole surgical team deep rooted family secrets, all about the crazies in my family, and let's say whatever else I said was enough to make *Super Doc* and the whole team crack up laughing and he was blushing like y'all wouldn't believe.

That's when I started coming out of it and waking up from my cat nap, because I heard them all burst out laughing and I see *Super Doc*'s fingers pulling down the blind just enough to show his cap & eyes and tell me to go back to sleep! I realized in my stupor I said something funny, but had no clue as to what it was. By now it's done and *Super Doc* had my left breast covered in a few small gauze bandages and I was being wheeled out into recovery...with a trail of laughter still coming from the OR and smirks from the recovery nurses.

Now it's my turn to blush beet red because apparently I'd committed some more faux pas in the OR and in order for all these women to keep looking at me it must've been something towards *Super Doc*. Great.

Realizing there was absolutely nothing I could do about it I decided to simply let it go. That lasted all of a few minutes until one of the nurses came by to take my temperature and blood pressure and yes, she was smirking at me, too. I begged her to tell me what I'd said or done in the OR and she just looked at me wide eyed and said the Vegas Rule applied – what happened in the OR stayed in the OR! Maybe I should be glad this surgery wasn't video tapped after all...

Naturally, the bandage just happened to fall off early...even though *Super Doc* reminded me that he'd see me in a week for a follow up appt and remove the bandage himself at his office. You know, they really should use better adhesive on bandages. I was ASTOUNDED at the difference and happier than I'd been in almost a year! He was able to remove the excess skin, shifting the implant and breast back into position and man-oh-man did the girls look good! I was tickled pink and so was Studly. The next surgery would only be in about 10 weeks we were told and by then we'd be able to see if the skin healed up enough for *Super Doc* to try to handle the nipple reconstructions in only one surgery. Again, I let him know I was in it with him til the end and whatever happened was going to happen. We'd be through when he said we were and not a moment sooner. Hey, I'm sorta' getting the hang of this patience thing.

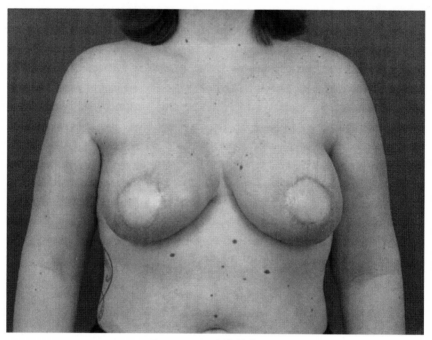
Position 1 / full front
Skin and muscles accepted permanent implants, excess skin removed from left breast allowing it to center and shape up nicely! Now my girls are both looking in the right direction!

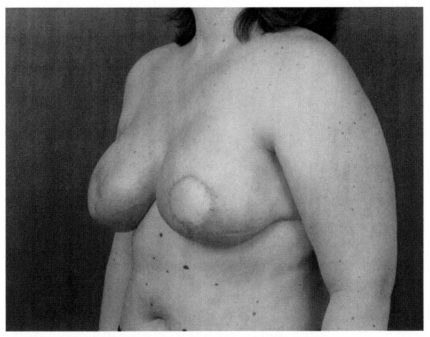

Position 2 / 45 degree angle of left side
Crease showing on the side of the left breast is where the bra
is becoming too tight. The girth of the permanent implants
is definitely larger than my natural breasts were!

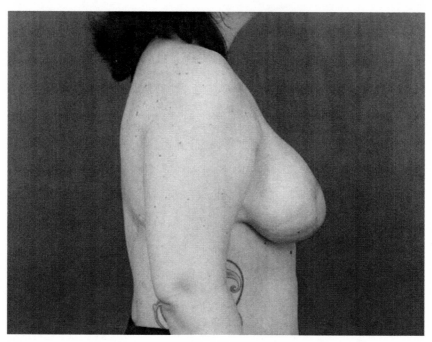

Position 6 / 90 degree angle of right side

# Taxes Happen

Everyone knows the old adage about how nothing is more certain than death and taxes. Well, ain't that the truth. A few years ago, we met an amazing tax rep from our local area. Let's call her Sassy Tax. When I walked into her office with my goody bag of W2s to every single medical receipt categorized, she threw both hands up stopping traffic and looked me in the eye asking what had happened. I explained that I'd been diagnosed last April with breast cancer, underwent a bilateral mastectomy, all the expansion procedures, and was almost done with my reconstruction.

She slowly grinned and fist bumped me. I didn't know that she was a breast cancer survivor of twenty seven years! She explained that back then technology naturally wasn't as hi-tech as it is now a days and when she'd had her bilateral mastectomy and tried to begin the reconstruction process it was simply too painful. She actually had the surgeon remove the expanders and she chose to go without breasts at all. Because of the pain and bad experiences, she had never tried again for breasts. She was cool with her decision, and let me tell you – it's a personal one as to how far you're willing to go or not. I totally understood where she was coming from.

After realizing I found another breast-friend, we hunkered down over all our tax documents and got to work. About an hour and a half later, Sassy Tax calculated that I would be able to deduct some, but not all of what we had to pay out of pocket in the past year for all these surgeries. Items like parking receipts, prescriptions, co-pays, and medical equipment were definitely working in our favor. Things like special pj's and clothing I had to buy in order to give doctor's easy access or back to work in were not. It just depends on how you work it and what kind of money is involved, right? Once our taxes were put together, I gave her a huge squeeze and made an appt to come back on the fourteenth to pay Uncle Sam.

Walking in a few weeks later one day ahead of the tax due date and grittin' my teeth knowing I'd have to write that check, here comes Sassy Tax telling me I had changed her mind after twenty-seven years, hearing about my experiences and how awesome my team of doctors were and she wanted to try for expanders and hopefully permanent implants again. "Seeing you inspires me," she said and that was all she wrote.

My dam broke and the dam tears busted loose ruining my dam makeup. It was all worth it though. No survivor had said that to me before, and it's one of the rare comments a person never forgets. Get you some green dollar signs tattooed on instead of nipples Sassy Tax, because you've certainly earned it!

# Nipple-licious

Surgery time once again rolled around and at *Super Doc*'s pre-op, he assured *Studly* and I that my skin had healed very well from the past surgery and it looked as if he'd be able to pull off the three surgeries in one operation like planned. Top that off with the fact he'd also finally be able to Lipo-suction underneath the scars on my back to relieve pressure and you have yourself the makings of a party! Woo-Hoo!

"Oh yeah, and this time I'm knocking you out" said *Super Doc*, with a mischievous grin on his face, "I can't have you telling secrets and embarrassing my surgical team in the OR again!"

Folks, I'll never live whatever that was down and *Super Doc* will never let me forget whatever it was I forgot.

Monday morning I got a phone call from the New-Kid-In-Town at *Super Doc*'s office, letting me know insurance had denied the referral from *Super Doc* stating the lipo-suction behind the back scars was indeed medically necessary and that we had saved that particular surgery until the very end because of the nature of the operation. After all, I was going on my tummy first so *Super Doc* could suck the fat that had built up behind my scars, he would stitch the back side up, flip me over, and then begin on the front. I was getting a double whammy. This wasn't fun, and it wasn't elected plastic surgery.

We're talking constant pressure and irritation on my scars bulging at the top halves, and me not once being able to lay flat in a bed for a whole year. After asking New-Kid-In-Town a few key questions I'd learned to ask about medical coding and billing, I let her know I would call her back by tomorrow at lunchtime. If I couldn't get insurance to understand and realize the situation, then I simply couldn't have this part of the operation at this point in time. I wasn't in agony over this, after all I'd made it a year and could make it a little longer until the medical bills were paid off and we'd just start anew with this last tid bit.

At least, that's what I was thinking about as a last resort. I was actually looking forward to busting my insurance rep for denying a claim that a doctor had even referred as medically necessary! I don't mind handling a little of *Super Doc*'s lightweight and apparently, I was spoiling for a good fight anyways. I made my phone calls and visited a few key offices that afternoon, then tried to remain calm while I was secretly antsy inside to see if I did the trick.

*Amazing Admin* called me the very next morning and before I could even get my "Hello?" out, she was chuckling at herself saying, "Get ready to tell me you love me!"

*Amazing Admin* not only called all declining parties involved, she went all the way up to the insurance agency's Medical Director and gnawed on his ear until he cried Uncle. Heck, I hadn't even gotten to that level yet. This is why she's the *Amazing Admin* – da-da-da-dum! Oh – I mean Ta-Ta-Ta-Tas!

When that Wednesday afternoon rolled around, the blue tattoos came out in full scale color flourishes. *Studly* helped me hold onto my hospital negligee while *Super Doc* went to work marking up my skin flaps where the nipples would go and the outlines around my back scars where the Lipo-suction would take place. Mama and Daddy happened to be in the room visiting before *Super Doc* walked in, so they got to see me in all my scarred-up-skin-flapped-glory.

Doesn't both me a bit it being Mama and Daddy, hell they made me and over the past year there isn't anything about the surgeries I haven't shown them. Some people might seem squeamish about that, but it's just what we do in my family. Scars give character, anyways! My Daddy being the Cop he is began asking the who's and how's of the surgery and I couldn't help but giggle when *Super Doc* looked straight at Daddy with a serious expression on his face and said, "It's Magic" which is his typical response to questions.

Then he actually showed Mama and Daddy in layman's terms how he would draw cross-hairs (like on a gun's scope) on the skin flap and take each quarter section and pinch up the excess skin. Once he'd stitched and glued the foundation in place, he could take the tips of the four-quarter triangle edges and fold them over step at a time while stitching and gluing with each fold. Nipple origami. Pretty cool, huh?

He even clued us all in as to what the bandages would look like for the nipple reconstruction which was different from anything else thus far in our adventures. Once the origami is complete, a clear plastic bubble surrounded by a thick spongy base with double-sided tape is sealed right over the nipple. The purpose of the hard plastic bubble is to act as a protector in case you were to bump into something, roll over in your sleep, etc. I like thinking I now totally understand the cup & jock strap thing, which cracks *Studly* up, but it's still the same principle!

For the Lipo-suction underneath the back scars, *Super Doc* told us he was going to make a small incision right on top of both existing scars so that it would simply blend in to what was there and not mark me any worse. I thought that was very thoughtful of him, after all a girl can only tell the Saber Toothed Tiger story so many times before people think you're acting tougher than you really are. He would inject a solution all around the area he was going to Lipo out because filling the area with liquid loosens up the fatty tissue. I could expect to feel very sore for a few days afterwards (what's new) and the skin might bruise deeply and even leak a little bit at the incision; however, all of that is normal. Now let's get this show on the road!

Rollin, rollin, rollin down towards the OR and I meet up with *Just Joe* the Anesthesiologist. He's a pretty cool doctor if I do say so myself and I was very comfortable with he and his assistant to the point where the assistants were already in the OR fussing because they hadn't had a chance to get a quick Coke from the cafeteria in between surgeries, and I teased them both that Mama and I checked out the café earlier and since they weren't serving Margarita's on Cinco de Mayo, then we just weren't interested. They all hee-hawed laughing and the teasing commenced. Next thing I know, Just Joe leans over me with a syringe and says, "Happy Cinco de Mayo, here's your margarita!" I woke up about three hours later. That margarita must've been Top Shelf.

It took me a while to wake up enough to actually focus on a face, which is sort of odd for me since I usually wake up kicking and pitching a hissy fit over whatever is in my doped up mind at the time. I just laid there and kept right on nodding off like it was the best nap I'd ever had. Finally, *Super Doc* came over and was shaking my foot saying, "Come on now – wake up and see my origami!" I did and my eyes got huge seeing actual nipples for the first time in a year on my body and man did they look really natural and pretty!

*Super Doc* had already went into the waiting room to speak to *Studly*, Mama and Daddy, then brought *Studly* back to sit with me while I was coming around. When I thought I was ready to actually get off the stretcher and into a chair I just jumped right up and then promptly sat my butt down. Good God, I was hurting like I couldn't believe from the Lipo on my back. I know I keep saying that it feels like I've been beat with a baseball bat, but that's the truth. Except this time, the bat was made out of metal and bigger than last time. I gingerly moved my arms around accepting the feelings and even though I knew it was cheesy, I just couldn't help but look down my own shirt at those pretty nipples! OK, so they're not going to look pretty to anyone other than the receiving person. Other people are only going to see the blood and Betadine stained skin under a plastic bubble. To me they were the most gorgeous things I'd seen in a whole year.

I sat in the chair, ate my Saltine crackers and drank my Ginger Ale like a good patient, complained that the Royal We had forgotten Nana's chicken salad again, and then they told me I was good enough to head on home as long as I took two pain pills before leaving. Fantastic. *Studly* helped me pull on 'our' favorite shirt and I stepped into comfy shorts & my favorite flops and we're hitting the road, Jack. Forgot my pillow to lean back against though; you'd think I would have this routine down pat by now. I should really start making a checklist of stuff. Anal retentive – who me?

Made it home and into my recliner, breathed a sigh of relief and woke up after a lil' nappy-poo to Nana coming in the door with her famous chicken salad. Life does not get much better than this. Her chicken salad is the miracle food when you're nauseous after surgery and your taste buds are off. It always hits the spot and makes you feel better! Nana just has the magic. Simple as that.

Guess what happened in the middle of the night waking me up? My neck was itching like crazy and I felt like the undersides of my boobs were sweating to death. Great – here comes the reaction to Anesthesia and a hot flash to boot. Reaction yes, hot flash no. I sprang right up out of the recliner and wasn't experiencing any pain at all, so I went upstairs to the bathroom for a cold washcloth. The minute my eyes adjusted to the light and I grabbed for the front of our favorite shirt I almost freaked out. It was covered in blood, not sweat. *Studly* is asleep still and I'm alone in the guest bathroom looking down at myself thinking OMG.

I unbuttoned our favorite shirt and took a deep breath thinking whatever happened, at least I didn't have any feeling to go along with it. Remember earlier then I talked about the thick spongy material and double-sided tape attaching the plastic bubble over the nipple? S-P-O-N-G-E. It's porous. Well, duh! And because the plastic bubble was hovering over the skin, your natural body temperature heats up and creates condensation. The sweat beads drop off the bubble and hit the dried blood turning it to wet blood, and voila – you sprung yourself a leak thru the sponge!

What a predicament. What do you do now, you ask? You keep wet wipes on hand for the first three to four days, and every once in a while take a swipe of that cool wipe against the under edge of the sponge and breast. It actually feels pretty refreshing if I do say so myself! By the fourth day, the leaking stopped although the plastic bubble still had a little bit of condensation visible. And after the initial pain pill at the hospital, I never had to take another one. Not one. Sure, I was sore on my back, but it wasn't anything major like it had been when I'd first woke up from the surgery. I literally didn't even take an aspirin, y'all. I was good to go.

Mama took me out on Friday afternoon so she could help me try on men's baggy button down dress shirts that would fit on top of bulky bandages and not look too totally sloppy. I knew I would need two things to make this happen: men's tank undershirts in dark colors and dark colored button ups. You don't wear light colored pants when you're on your menstrual cycle, so the same principle applied in my mind – I didn't want to spring a leak at work in light colored clothes. Especially when you work in an office full of older military men that do not understand what to do with me even when I'm healthy. So, tank undershirts to act as the first barrier to catch leaks and adding padding over my cup, (no jock strap applied since a strap across my back scars and lipo'd area was not in the future.) The outer shirt to hang loose camouflaging the plastic bubbles even further and simply being comfy.

When we'd finished shopping, I went home with a pack of Hanes tanks and six button down shirts. Works for me, since I had planned on donating them when I was finished with healing and using it as a tax write off – now y'all have to admit, that's creative! I can't wait to surprise Sassy Tax with this next season, hehehe!

# Girls Night In

I had a few girlfriends over Friday night, which turned into quite a shindig. After each of the surgeries thus far, we either had a girl's night, movie night, doing nothing night – didn't matter what kind of night it was as long as I had my girlfriends close by. Boys are not allowed in the clubhouse because they do not know the secret handshake or the super secret password. On that night, the boys have their own night usually belly-up'd at the favorite bar. When the girls roll in, you know it. Whew – hair is let down, shoes not allowed and dropped at the door, beer is ice cold and the gossip is the best ever each and every time!

This go-round, we happened to add a new addition to the tight circle of friends and she's Hyper-Chic. Good lord, if you think I'm sarcastic and hyperactive I can't wait til you get a load of her! She barrels in kicking off her flops, ripping loose a messy ponytail, holding onto her already popped top long neck raised high, with her left arm wrapped around a case of beer and shouting, "Here's to nipples!" I thought I was going to fall out of my recliner I was laughing so hard. She so fits into our circle of friends. She simply rocks and that's all there is to it.

It didn't take this gaggle of giggling girls to pop the question I knew they were dying to ask. Can we see them? You know, I honestly thought about dropping my top so they could get a good shock and see just how 'real' life had been to my body over the past year. But I didn't want them looking at my permanently perky new nipples just yet. Even though they could've handled it alright once the shock value wore off and I had explained all the major details, I simply wanted the party to remain at an upbeat and fun level…none of us really wanted a dose of reality or go through too real emotions tonight. So instead of showing them, I decided to have a lil fun.

"Shhh, listen to this" I said getting their attention and I reached up and used my fingernail to tap-tap-tap hard on the plastic bubble.

Every jaw dropped in the room and a round of WTF's and OMG's were shouted out and hysterical laughter bubbled out of everyone! They had no idea I had plastic bubbles around the nipples, and they thought the sound was for real – I let them all squeal and shout for a few seconds while I once again caught my breath from laughing so hard and then explained to them what it really was.

Hyper-Chic was dumbfounded, and she was also the one sitting closest to me at my feet on the floor. She couldn't help herself, she just reached up like she was about to tap on the bubbles and I let her get within a fine frog hair of actually touching the bubble, and I let loose a screaming OUCH that had her jumping about three feet off the floor and screaming in horror right back at me until she realized she hadn't even touched me! Man it was awesome – I got her good that time!

The next thing we knew, it was close to midnight and all the pizza had been eaten already so fried bologna sandwiches was the general craving for the moment. Off to the nearest twenty-four hour grocery store two of them went to gather food for the rest of the tribe and thirty minutes later FBS were thoroughly analyzed, mysteries solved, and served on paper plates. At some point in time everyone crashed out in sleeping bags, recliners or on the floor. By the time I woke up the next morning only one remained stuck to my floor like silly putty.

I tell you what, I absolutely love my girls. Through good times and bad, a select few remain true – when you finally figure out who they are, try your best to do them right and never let them go. Besides, by that time they'll know too many of your secrets!

Monday morning rolled around like the bad habit they are, and I woke up hearing dwarfs in my head. Time to wake up to another sponge bath and slip into my new work shirts. After all, we got a business to run! I made it less than half a day and had to call in reinforcements. After the long weekend I still felt like I was trying to wake up from the anesthesia I was so foggy. The only thing I could think of was that this past surgery marked the fifth time in eleven months I had underwent some sort of anesthesia and my body just wasn't cooperating. I noticed mistakes I was making at work only after they were made, Mama said I would start talking and drift off in midsentence, and it might take me a trip or two through the house to figure out what in the world I was looking for. If it was happening to someone else I knew I'd just laugh, but it was becoming downright aggravating...I think.

Thursday afternoon I danced into *Super Doc*'s office and couldn't wait to tell him I'd not had a single pain pill, I hadn't bruised hardly at all, and I was ready to bust him with a line I'd been thinking of all weekend long because I knew it'd make him laugh.

"Doc, you gotta do something about the condensation of a new nation, these cups are making my new nipples look like Waffle House windows in summertime!"

It just cracks *Super Doc* and *Amazing Admin* up when I act like a backwoods brunette, especially when I know they've had a long day. We stroll on back to my room in *Super Doc*'s office and before I could even get the shirts off and disposable kimono on here he comes busting in, walks right up to me with eyes as big as saucers and says, "I can't believe you! I knocked you out this time for surgery and you still ran your mouth in the OR! Do you know what you said this time?"

Honey, I thought I was going to die because I knew there was no way in hell I could have woken up from *Just Joe's* Margarita Anesthesia – I had about a seconds worth of Oh, Shit panic and then I doubled over laughing! It went downhill from there. Mama just happened to be with me for the unveiling and she smacks one back at him saying, "I brought your Baby Boy a pygmy goat from our herd. *Amazing Admin* is holding him now, but we brought a carry crate for you to take him home in."

Talk about someone being dumbfounded. *Super Doc's* eye's bug right out of his head and goes, "Oh, no you didn't! Did you really? Well… uhhh" and he couldn't figure out a way to tell her there was no way he was taking home that baby goat, or rather that Mrs. Doc would have the locks changed before that happened.

We busted out laughing all over again, and y'all would've thought that's all we were going to do was sit around my room and bust jokes on each other. *Super Doc* even took a picture of me in the cups before the unveiling so y'all can really understand just what it looks like. Bless Her Heart, the new intern, didn't know what to make of this scene. *Amazing Admin* had given her the scoop on what all had transpired over the course of the year with my procedures and progress; however, I don't think she prepared Bless Her Heart for blunders in the OR, pygmy goats, pics for the book or our shenanigans!

We all finally caught our breath from laughing and *Super Doc* leaned the exam chair back telling me to, "Hold this for me" and laying all the fresh gauze right in between my boobs. Well, they do make a good shelf! Off come the sponge and plastic bubbles and OMG were they awesome! *Super Doc* used some of his magic to get the gunk off, let me know it might take a week or so for the scabs to come off on its own and not to force it, slapped that fresh gauze on with a piece of tape and said, "Have fun washing & looking at 'em; I'll see you in a month!"

Bless Her Heart was so flabbergasted she forgot to take my blood pressure and temperature and had to knock on the door to come back in for the readings. I sure hope she sticks with *Super Doc* so she'll know what *excellence* and *good* really look like. And if her karma and stars are aligned, she just might have the privilege of working for *Super Doc* one day.

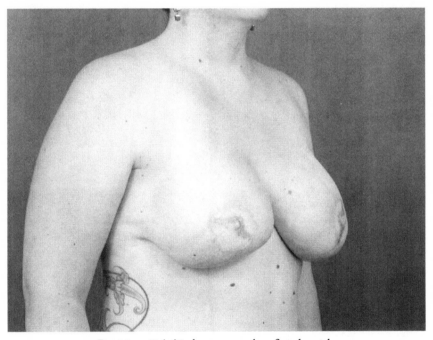

Position 7 / 45 degree angle of right side
Post nipple reconstruction
Head lights on high beam – WHOOO-HOOO!

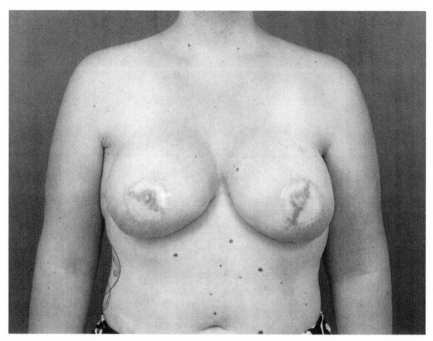

Position 1 / full front
Very pleased with results!

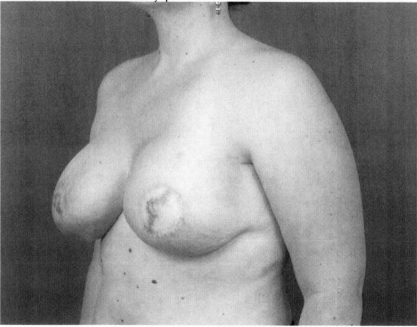

Position 2 / 45 degree angle of left side

*Amazing Admin* was waiting for me as I walked around to her checkout counter, grinning from ear to ear and bouncing in her seat just waiting for me. "Well, well, well? What'd you think? Didn't I tell you this was the fun part?"

She was exactly right, this was the most fun I'd had taking bandages off in a year. I was through with surgeries. The last bandage had been shucked. *Amazing Admin* and I looked at each other, still grinning and giggling, while she made the next appointment and said, "I can't believe that was the last major ordeal and pretty soon we won't have to see you in the office anymore."

I was so excited I ran through the front door of our home and peeled back that teeny little piece of gauze & tape to show *Studly* just how incredible my new nipples looked. Before I could even tell him what all transpired at *Super Doc*'s, I looked up into his eyes and he was just as teary as I was. We both laughed at each other through the tears and knew it was almost over with. Sweet Jesus, it was almost over with. We couldn't wait to get upstairs and use a lil' Peroxide and soap to clean up what gunk we could. Once the top layer was shed, I could see a whole lot of soft pink nipple that never looked so good! This was better than any prize in the cereal box because they were here to stay. First thing I did was toss on a sexy lil' number and flash my *Studly* out on the deck!

Y'all, someone once asked me what the secret was to marriage and I promise you this – when the gross stuff becomes romantic, you know you've got it made. That is our secret to marriage. Knowing that even at your worst, your partner is there with you every single step of the way – letting you lean on them for support with shocking news, patient while you both weigh out the options, kissing you good-bye each and every single time as you're wheeled off to surgery and kissing you when you wake up fighting from Anesthesia, wiping your butt when you can't, handling drain tubes and pouches like they were no big deal, watching your body go from something out of a horror movie into a beautiful transition, helping you ever so gently wash off the scabby gunk and telling you that you're beautiful every step of the way, willing to come back for more, and knowing that if the shoe was on the other foot you would do the same no questions asked – now *that* is a marriage. Besides, I trim his ear hair and love bullfrogs that croak under our covers...that's true love!

# Ink Does A Body Good ~
## *Tattooing the nipple and areola*

One month past Cinco de Mayo, I roll in for my check up. *Super Doc* was excited to see *Studly* and I, and I got to clue him in on finding a publisher for this book! His eyes about popped right out of his head and he was just as thrilled as we were. I promised him an unedited version of his very own to read through, critique, and let me know if something didn't quite suit his sensibilities. Of course, he just laughed and promised me he'd give it a thorough scrubbing and if I was lucky a forward or review! We made a trip to the paparazzi room for a lil' flash-time, then he and New Kid in Town told me the tattoo artist was in the house.

Now, I was pretty excited to get to meet the permanent cosmetic tattoo artist – after all, I've had my eyeliner permanently tattooed a little over 6 yrs ago and I also have my big tattoo on my hip that *Super Doc* was so careful not to bother and I was honestly interested to see just how her procedure would be different than a normal tattoo.

Turns out, Inkerbell personally uses an organic ink. The reason why she said was because normal tattoo ink has zinc-oxide (metal flakes) in the liquid and any future MRIs I had could possibly burn my skin or create discoloration of the pigment. Organic ink has no metal flakes and therefore would be better in the long run. Inkerbell also had an entire flyer full of areola colors to choose from. Her flyer showed squares of organic ink like paint chips from Home Depot, and dang if we didn't see a shade similar to my original nipple color!

She gave us an idea to think about; using the color named 'natural nipple' would allow a darker shade of a nude-pink tint that wouldn't be viewable through a white cotton shirt with no bra underneath. Truthfully, when your girls are perky and firm, you don't have to wear a bra. What a concept! And the idea of being au-natural underneath play clothes was appealing. If nothing else, we have plenty of colors to think about and choose from over the next two months before the tattooing.

The after-care for the nipple tattooing was standard as normal tattooing – the first week's color would be very bold, antibacterial soap & ointment until the top layer of skin began to flake off, no chlorine from a swimming pool for a few weeks because it could possibly dilute the color, and in eight weeks if I found pigments that didn't take or dead-spots in the color as I call them, then she could apply a bit of touch-up. Voila!

Tattooing first week of Sept. 2010

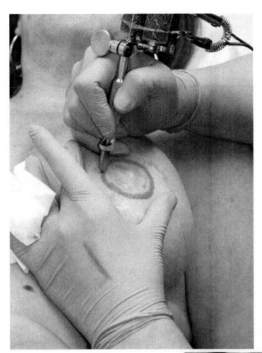

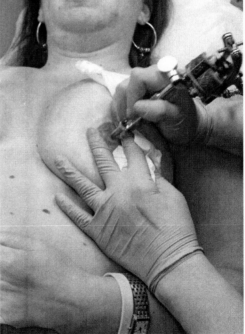

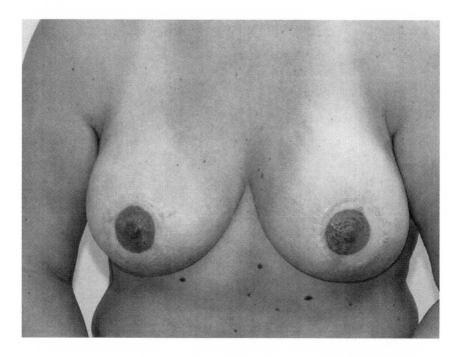

All of a sudden, it *really* hit me. That was the last surgery. All that was left was next month's check up and the tattoos would be it. It's going to be over. I won't see *Amazing Admin* or *Super Doc* anymore after that, unless I'm really lucky and we see each other outside of the office. I won't have *Super Doc* anymore.

O-H-M-Y-G-O-D.

I had never realized until this moment just how much I had depended on *Super Doc* and *Amazing Admin*. They had literally been our universe for the whole past year and they were about to leave because their work would be done. Y'all, I started squalling like a baby before we were even out of the parking lot. I was reminded of one of those chain email poems you get from friends & family that talk about how people come into your life for a reason, a season or a lifetime and that each phase is unique in its own way not only because of the who's and why's someone enters your life, but because of the end of the phase.

The world doesn't stop turning while you're in pain or recuperating. Bills still have to be paid, storms are still going to knock over trees in the yard, jealous ex's you haven't given a second thought to will always be petty despite what you're going through, and garage door openers are still going to fall on your head when you least expect it. It's just another day in paradise, and you're going to get through it just fine.

*Super Doc* has other people to save, hope to restore, and self-esteem to raise. *Amazing Admin* has another patient's insurance Medical Director to gnaw on. It's time for me to let them go do their Magic and give up my room. They are out to defend the good people in their white coats and scrubs, and kick cancer's ass!

# A Reason, A Season, or a Lifetime

People come into your life for a reason, a season, or
a lifetime. When you figure out which one it is, you
will know what to do for each person.
When someone is in your life for a REASON . . . It is
usually to meet a need you have expressed. They have
come to assist you through a difficulty, to provide you
with guidance and support, to aid you physically,
emotionally, or spiritually. They may seem like a
godsend, and they are! They are there for the reason
you need them to be.
Then, without any wrongdoing on your part, or at an
inconvenient time, this person will say or do something
to bring the relationship to an end.
Sometimes they die.
Sometimes they walk away.
Sometimes they act up and force you to take a stand.
What we must realize is that our need has been met, our
desire fulfilled, their work is done. The prayer you
sent up has been answered. Now it is time to move on.

When people come into your life for a SEASON . . .
Because your turn has come to share, grow, or learn.
They bring you an experience of peace, or make you laugh.
They may teach you something you have never done.
They usually give you an unbelievable amount
of joy. Believe it! It is real! But, only for a season.

LIFETIME relationships teach you lifetime lessons; things
you must build upon in order to have a solid emotional
foundation. Your job is to accept the lesson, love the
person, and put what you have learned to use in all
other relationships and areas of your life. It is said
that love is blind but friendship is clairvoyant.

# Afterword

*Nana's Chicken Salad Recipe*

- 3 to 4 cans of chicken breast chopped or fresh cooked chicken of equal amounts
- 4 stalks of celery chopped
- 1 large onion
- Several Tbs of pickle relish
- To taste: black pepper, poppy seeds and Duke's mayonnaise

*Medicinal Margaritas*

- With a shot of orange juice
- Zippity-do-da-straws

*Tool Box*

- Long handled shower sponge
- No Rinse Shampoo
- Shower chair
- Button front pajama's
- Prayer Shawl
- Slip on shoes
- Baggy tanks and button front shirt

# About The Author

Melissa Brumbelow was diagnosed with BRCA1, a genetic form of breast cancer, in April 2009. Facing treatment decisions and multiple major surgeries, she chose to document her experiences to help others. She is a lifelong resident of Douglasville, Georgia, where she lives with her family.

LaVergne, TN USA
30 December 2010
210642LV00004B/4/P